MW00622769

Seeking a Life
Out of Pennsylvania's Mill Hunky Madness

DAVID BRAYSHAW

SEEKING A LIFE
OUT OF PENNSYLVANIA'S MILL HUNKY MADNESS

Print ISBN: 978-1-66789-753-0
eBook ISBN: 978-1-66789-754-7

Contents

CHAPTER 1

I was eleven years old when my mother made her first attempt to kill herself.

It really shouldn't have been a surprise to me, my twin brother Denny, or to my younger brother Doug and my older sister Diana. For several months, Mom had been displaying odd behaviors, like sitting for hours in the dark basement shower with the water on, declaring that invisible beings were out to hurt her, running stark naked to the next-door neighbor's house, and rarely making any sense while talking.

Then, one early Pennsylvania morning, I heard my twin brother Denny yelling in horror. Still half asleep, I first thought the house was on fire. That was understandable. A fire had already caused us to lose a previous home after a coal furnace door had been left ajar. Then, I'd had to leap from a second-floor window and be caught by firemen. We lost everything, even though my family possessed very little to lose. In a way, for a five-year-old boy, it was fun watching firemen extinguish the flames as we stood in the cold, clad only in our pajamas and wrapped in blankets.

This time, I just heard the screams. "It's Mom. She's hung herself," Denny yelled. For a second, I was stunned but managed to run toward Denny, who was still screaming. Doug and Diana stood motionless near the table in the living room, clearly frightened.

My father ran into the room and yelled to Diana, Doug, and me to stay out of the way. The son of a hard-working, hard-drinking railroad worker,

Dad didn't know how to show affection. He knew how to give orders. "Denny," he shouted, "get your brothers and sister to sit on that couch near the door."

"Don't move. Stay there," he commanded and then frantically raced up the staircase to the framed upper level. We found out later what happened. He had pushed aside the sheet of plastic over the entryway to the floor. My mother dangled from a rafter with the type of rope used to hang clothes outdoors to dry. It was a hard, plastic-coated line whose coating kept it from decaying in the weather. A portion was still around her neck, which Dad removed. Her feet were a few inches from the floor next to a chair she'd used as a launching point.

Dad used his pocketknife to hack at the rope Mom used to hang herself. Frustrated by the slow rate of speed it took to cut the line, my father, being a muscular man, ripped it apart with his hands. Mom toppled onto the level that served as both the first floor and basement ceiling and was placed by Dad onto the couch.

While we sat shivering from the cold and fear, feeling alien, out of place, in another world, Dad ordered Diana to call an ambulance. She scurried to the phone.

"Is she dead?" I kept asking. No one answered. I could see Mom lying motionless, not seeming to breathe. The remains of the cord still clung to her neck.

All I could think of was the last conversation I'd had with her. The previous day, she had sent me to the neighborhood store to buy a gallon of milk. "The milk won't be more than fifty cents," she'd said, "so get some candy to share with your sister and brothers." She'd handed me a dollar. With an unusually tight grasp, she hugged me. "You know I love you very much, Dave. You're a good boy. You do what you're told with few complaints. My love for you is forever."

Those words now sounded like a goodbye. Were they?

Dad leaned over her. I could see him trying to pull out her tongue. He told Denny to bring him a spoon. "If this doesn't work, I may have to pin her tongue to her cheek."

"I smell something," Denny announced. "There's an odor! Does anyone else smell it?"

"It's propane gas," Dad decided. "Shut it off."

My twin hurried to the stove. I was sent to open the front door. The cool wind kept trying to shut it. I finally got a concrete block from the garage and turned it into a doorstop.

Trying to help, I suggested getting a fan to dissipate the fumes. Dad nodded. In the basement, I found the square blower and plugged it in behind the couch.

An eternity passed, and still no ambulance. Diana called again. The ambulance drivers had been erroneously sent to Franklin Avenue in Aliquippa, several miles from my family's home in Monaca.

The driver of the ambulance was told by the operator to drive to Franklin Avenue, and since that street name was a dominant, often-used road in Aliquippa, that is where he assumed he was being sent. Monaca's Franklin Avenue was located on the right side of a large hill called Sylvan Crest, on which were single-story, blue-collar houses, mostly built between the 1930s and 1950s.

When our family first moved in, it had just been an open basement. The attic where Mom had hung herself, the first floor, and the flat roof were completed later. Dad's initial intent had been to complete the top portion, but his lack of funds and motivation kept us in that cellar, minus bathroom facilities and interior walls, for seven years. Thin curtains surrounded Dad and Mom's bed, while we four kids had no boundaries.

Daily, Dad carried a five-gallon bucket to the backyard, which he dumped into a deep pit. A piece of plywood covered the opening. He was then in his early thirties and willing to live in a cave, which is about what we had.

On the basement wall, Dad nailed a black iron sign with white letters that read, "I used to cry because I had no shoes until I met a man who had no feet." I believe those words were meant to keep us thankful while living in an underground, windowless block box.

Dad kept rubbing Mom's cheeks and encouraging her. "Stay with me," he pleaded, showing more emotion in those few minutes than he ever had in all his kids' lives. To me, seeing him so distraught was almost as bad as what Mom did.

Finally, I heard a siren. Two Emergency Medical Technicians charged into the house with a rolling gurney. I could see that Mom was breathing. They checked her pulse, lifted her eyelids, and looked at her eyes. Mom did not respond. They lifted her onto the gurney. She seemed to make some simple noises.

We watched them roll her out the door to the waiting ambulance. We stood in the doorway and watched as the white ambulance hurried away with siren blaring and lights flashing.

My father closed the door. "Nobody knows what happened here, kids. Do you hear me?" he insisted. No words of comfort. He was more concerned about what the neighbors would think. "Nobody, and I mean nobody."

Until Dad could get someone to watch over his children, he was content to permit the techs to oversee Mom's needs. In a matter of a few hours, one of his female friends, the daughter of a fellow mill worker, received Dad's call. Darla was a sweet and caring woman, perhaps eight to ten years older than me. To Dad, she was special and immensely cooperative.

My promised silence lasted for many years. I didn't even tell anyone that my mom survived. After recovering, she was placed in Dixmont State Hospital. For two years, my father drove there every Saturday to see her.

I didn't find out why she tried to take her own life until decades later.

Prior to the suicide attempt, Dad had set up an appointment for Mom to see a psychiatrist. The doctor recommended that Mom be sent to Dixmont the next day. Feeling she was destined to lose her children if she gave in to psychiatric treatment, which in those days was deeply frowned upon by society, she chose to try to end her life. I knew nothing about her being told to undergo psychiatric treatment. I learned this from my sister's conversations with Mom's mother, Celia.

I didn't tell anyone about what happened that night until I was in my twenties and a member of the U.S. Navy. I didn't intend to break this secret, but I was doing some laundry when I overheard a civil service secretary tearfully tell strangers that her father had just shot her mother.

I walked up to her and asked if she needed to talk. That was when I told her what had happened to my mother, one of an ongoing series of tragedies that have marked my life.

"I know it hurts," I told her. "It hurts like hell. Whether it ends with good news or bad, you will survive. You will go on with your life."

She hugged me and didn't want to let go.

From that time on, I found it easier to share my family trauma. Still, to this day, although more than sixty years have passed, I continue to heal, bit by bit.

Within a couple of years of Mom's institutionalization, my father decided to find a new mother for his children. I could not have anticipated that his pursuit of a replacement for Mom would be an undereducated, hillbilly alcoholic who would drive us from one residence and create even worse trauma than a fire or even a near suicide.

CHAPTER 2:

Leaving for Parma

By this time, Mom had been in the Dixmont State Hospital for two years. Every Saturday morning, at about 9 or 10 a.m., Dad drove his four kids to Mom's mother's apartment in Rochester while he visited Mom. We called her Nana Celia. She insisted we use that name, Nana, which I seldom heard used by other families until later in life. The long stairwell leading to her doorway, at the back side of a three-story building, I'll never forget. Always awaiting our attention as we entered her place was a candy dish filled with various treats, all of which we'd eat during our stay while Dad drove toward Pittsburgh to the asylum to see Mom.

A few times within those couple of years, Dad would take us along with him. At the rear of a six or seven-floor building, we parked and were told to look up at one of the upper-floor windows to see if we could catch sight of Mom. I don't remember seeing her. Maybe one of the others did.

Normally, the agenda for the day was to give each of us less than a dollar for entrance into either the Oriental or Family Theaters on Hines Street to watch a movie. I have many memories of both theaters.

Fifteen cents got us into the building, with a dime left for two candy bars or popcorn. Those were the days of scary movies like *The Tingler, The Wolfman, The Day the Earth Stood Still, Dracula, The Fly, The Mummy, The*

Blob, Frankenstein, and *Strait Jacket,* featuring actors like Boris Karloff, Vincent Price, and Joan Crawford, as well as John Wayne westerns, *Zorro, Lone Ranger,* and *The Graduate.* So fearful *Strait Jacket* made Denny after viewing about ten minutes of Joan Crawford's film, he ran out the door, down Hines Street, then up the Virginia Avenue hill, back to Nana Celia's apartment, before the end of the film.

When not at the movies, we were given enough money to bowl at Beaver Valley Bowl in Rochester, located at the bottom of Virginia Avenue next to the Ohio River and across a wide yard of railroad tracks. Eventually, we became impressive young bowlers, always with the need to find a properly fitting ball, which was the key to a good release. We never owned our own balls and always rented shoes.

One day, as best as I recall, in the winter months, Dad brought home with him a short, reasonably attractive woman from the poor, redneck, alcohol-laden town in Southeastern Missouri called Parma. Her name was Lula Mae Eiceman. Everyone called her Lou. Almost immediately, it was easy to see that alcohol would pose profound problems in our lives. When drinking, the two of them would always argue.

This afternoon, Denny and I were outside playing baseball at the Nixon field, unaware of what was taking place at home. The game was in the last of the ninth inning. We were winning and hungry, so we quit to get a bite to eat. Little did I know our lives were again about to change dramatically.

By the time Mom had been interred for two years, Dad had grown tired of not having a woman in his life, and tired of hopping from bed to bed. This newest woman he introduced us to had now moved into the basement with us. The two of them drank a lot and argued incessantly. After the game, upon entering the basement, I turned to Denny and asked, "Where is everybody? Shouldn't Lou, Diana, and Doug be home?" There was no sign of them in the cellar.

Earlier, as we were walking out the door with gloves in hand, ready for a ball game with the usual boys from Sylvan Crest, I'd heard the *Hi-Q* music theme, the prelude to the clay-animated children's television series *Davey and Goliath*. It was the favorite show of my six-year-old brother, Doug, who had been sitting on the floor with his eyes glued to the set. My fourteen-year-old sister, Diana, I had noticed a second earlier excitedly examining a new makeup kit her girlfriend, whose parents, strict conservatives and anti-fad, would not permit her to keep. Lou was out of sight.

Not until Dad arrived home a couple of hours later with a drinking buddy of his named Pete was Lou's note found scribbled on a telephone pad, informing Dad that she was taking both his children with her. If he wanted them returned, he'd have to come to get them.

Dad then erupted, "That's got to be one of the stupidest women on earth. Why would she take them? If she wanted to see her father, she could have gone alone. What purpose does it serve to take my kids?" It was one of the few times in my life I heard him speak with some semblance of parental care.

We would later learn that Lou had convinced Diana and Doug to grab some clothes and get into her car. She and Dad had agreed to this trip the night before, she'd told them. The destination was a small, one-traffic-light, countrified cotton town in Southeast Missouri called Parma, her childhood home.

As I view it today, Dad should have immediately called the police and had her charged with kidnapping. But he didn't. All through my life, I have remained astounded by Dad's decision not to have Lou arrested. It would have saved us so much torment and grief. Did she have something on him, something she threatened to go to the police with if he didn't follow her lead? What kept Dad clinging to this woman?

This was at that moment that Dad gave up his dream of completing our home. To him, it was time to let it go. He was eleven thousand dollars in debt and was holding on to a burden he hated. So, he handed the basement keys to his brother, Buzzy, to sell the house, and after ordering us to pack no more than a few sets of clothes, he told Denny and me, "Get into the car. Now!" So we did, and one of Dad's workmates, Pete, went with us.

All of the furniture, kitchenware, bunk beds, carpets, and anything else that made a home we left behind.

"Where are we headed now?" I asked Dad, so fed up with extreme behaviors. "What's this all about?" I didn't want to leave Sylvan Crest and was upset. I had plenty of friends there. It was home to me.

"We're on our way to get your brother and sister," he said as he backed out the car, still attired in his work clothes and unshowered.

Neither my brother nor I understood the full meaning of this. It was the tone of Dad's voice, together with his words, "we're on our way," that intimated we were in for another unbearable ordeal. This was the beginning of what we were about to witness for years to come, the combining of two whackos with the explosive natures of a brawling alcoholic and a potentially protective yet terribly misdirected, anxiety-filled father.

I've known more men who refused to contend with life's challenges without a female partner than I have men who endured hardships purely on their own. The son of a close friend in Pennsylvania hung himself after his wife declared their marriage finished. Men will search the online want-ads, go to bars, and attend churches in their hunt for a woman, not knowing anything about them, yet willing to blindly give all that they've earned just to get a compliant nod, even while they're ignorant of the full picture.

Dad's search for a homemaker, cook, and bed partner was habitual, void of vetting, and caused emotional harm to those around him. Barely middle-aged, his behavior resembled that of a man wrestling with a middle-aged crisis. He had to have Lou in his life even if she was sent by the devil himself. What was his attraction? Her cooking? For she was, without a doubt, a phenomenally gifted cook. On good days, she made dishes I never knew existed, so appetizingly good they tasted. Sauerkraut, pork, and potato dumplings with lemon meringue pie for dessert. Her breakfasts were top-of-the-line and included eggs, bacon, fried potatoes, and grits, with strong percolated coffee. Leftover greasy ingredients were poured into Crisco cans that sat on the stovetop, which she used in most dishes. She liked to fry.

On a routine basis, almost every afternoon and evening, Dad would find her mind entirely altered as she sat for hours at a bar shaping her personality into an uncontrollable wickedness.

Did Dad not realize he was placing his family in harm's way merely to satisfy his misguided need for food and whatever form of companionship that pretended to welcome him and his family? To Dad, Lou represented misplaced emotion. He should have been discerning. He should have thought of us first, but he didn't. No matter the personality of that woman, Dad refused to see things as they truly were. Lou's true nature was being fully exposed as a drunken kidnapper of weak and defenseless children.

In sheer disbelief, I sat in the rear seat of the station wagon still headed south, with Pete chaperoning with a cigarette between his fingers and singing "There Goes My Everything." Where, in God's name, were we headed? What is Parma? I thought Dad was about to involve himself in an aggressive criminal act. Would there be gunplay? Is that why Pete was with us?

"What are you going to do, Dad?" I insisted upon knowing. My mind was filled with many possibilities. At the same time, Denny and I had a few important baseball games lined up on Sylvan Crest, or The Hill. There were three neighborhood teams. None of us wore anything fancy, no uniforms, just our everyday clothes, for we were poor and entirely unsponsored. Three games were lined up for which we would be no-shows. I was desperate to get back to Monaca, Pennsylvania. In all the years we'd played baseball, we'd never missed a competition, never forfeited due to not showing. This was a first, and it bothered me. I badly wanted to win. I knew we could beat them after all the practice we'd put in catching flies, line drives, and grounders. We also gave the best man, our catcher, plenty of practice. He was a solid-bodied boy named Frank. His position wasn't a highly sought-after one because base runners headed for home ran over the brave ones.

Frank was given a new mitt by his father, and we excitedly looked forward to watching his performance. No fathers, most of whom were mill workers who preferred to sit at the same stools in their favorite fraternal organization, ever attended. It was just the kids on Sylvan Crest, the nickname of which still is The Hill, who played ball. An outstanding gesture was to see any adult male watching our games, whether he was related to any one of us or not. We played our best with eyes on us.

"We have to get your sister and brother back. Lou's taken them to Missouri," Dad said. I was all in favor of rescuing my siblings and sensed there was no promise of a quick and harmless rescue. We would grab them and get out; I hoped that was the plan, nothing more.

In the late evening, into Parma, Dad drove. We were kindly welcomed by Lou's father and sister and were given beds for the night. In the morning, I envisioned, we would be back on the road, headed for our ball games.

Pennsylvania law stated, at that time, that a person whose spouse was confined in a mental institution for three years could automatically apply for a divorce. This, I believe, may have been the motivation for this move. Dad was planning to marry this appalling alcoholic; all he needed was to wait out the remaining twelve months. But then, why not stay in Pennsylvania?

I was convinced Dad and Lou must have talked about leaving the Keystone State and didn't want to tell us. Lou refused any further delays and rushed her plans, taking the initiative to flee in a way that would force Dad to chase after her. Whatever their discussions, if indeed any took place, Lou, without Dad's approval, lied to two vulnerable kids. She fabricated a most unlikely story by telling Diana and Doug that she and Dad decided to move to Parma, a location surrounded by dirt roads, ditches, cotton fields, and farm vehicles, with a population of just over 1000. Now, how unlikely would that be, Dad consenting without ever being in Missouri, much less some unappealing hick town?

I thought again of my baseball commitments. "We had repeated wins. Double plays were happening more, and I was throwing great pitches," I lamented. "I can't see John pitching for me. He's too wild. We're going to lose all those games coming up," I declared, desperate for a U-turn. But we kept in a southwestern direction.

Eventually, our trip to Parma was filled with laughter and disgust over having to put up with Pete's stinking feet that reeked so badly the windows had to be lowered. A shower he likely hadn't taken for two weeks, he was at least a week unshaven and wore clothes suited for a bum. His shirt was torn below the rear portion of his collar. Little strength would be needed to rip it down the back. Did he have a suitcase? I didn't know.

Why Dad chose him to tag along was a mystery to me. Maybe it was his expressions, as Pennsylvania sarcasm is a binding language, ideal for redneck slang. I remember we talked about the TV show *Peter Gunn*, a private eye. Pete kept singing the show's theme song. In the end, we had a good bit of fun getting to Missouri as Pete took the brunt of the comments. Plus, boys think farting is funny, all of which we engaged in.

All that we owned we left behind in Pennsylvania. Who does that, but a couple of maniacs? Who would take off with nothing more than a couple of changes of clothes on a trip that would last for years?

Arriving at the Parma residence, I noticed the faded outer wood. It was two stories high and was situated with the front porch facing a set of railroad tracks. It had three bedrooms, and a backyard shed, and behind it were two hunting dogs in kennels. It was a relief to have arrived. The tracks led to the town's cotton gin mill. To the right side of the house was Lou's father's scrap metal yard. He was a good man, gentle and courteous, and, in a tender manner, asked that we call him Grampap.

There would never come a U-turn as the powers kept us in Parma. But after meeting Grampap, I was convinced I wanted to stay. The deep longing I had for love was met in him.

The first alcohol-produced fight I recall took place there, at the front of Grampap's house. We were not long there when Lou drove up one day in a brand new, bright red truck, drunk and out of her mind.

"We barely have a friggin' cent to get by from one day to the next," Dad loudly declared, "and here you come back with this shit!"

"I bought it for you," Lou replied loudly, "It's your damned Christmas present!"

Furious, he scolded, "You are truly one brainless, stupid bitch. What have you gotten me into?"

There was no way to make payments on such a vehicle. Dad had not yet found work as a welder and could barely afford a thirty-five-cent pack of Pall Malls.

"You're a no-good asshole," Lou replied. "You, and your damned kids, you're all a bunch of ungrateful bastards," she added as she rushed into her father's scrap yard to retrieve a heavy car generator that she repeatedly threw at the truck. The house was located a block from Main Street behind a family store on North Railroad Street. Other homes aligned the house on the northern part of the road. Residents heard the yelling and walked onto Railroad Street to look in our direction. This would soon become familiar behavior. At every residence Dad unloaded his family, police would, before long, investigate repeated disturbances, eventually demanding we pack up and leave their town.

Dad drove the vehicle back to the dealer, insisting it was parked in town and vandalized, which, I assume, kept him from paying damages.

Increasingly, behaviors went well beyond simple arguments. They used hostile strategies against each other. This first very public episode left me feeling distraught and hopeless. On the bright side, their fighting episodes I would not have to endure much longer, but not my brothers and sister. Desperate feelings for them would triple in quantity as days, weeks and months passed.

CHAPTER 3:

Living at Grampap's

The Catrons, Lou's family abiding in that home, made up of her father (Frank or Grampap), sister (Helen), and niece (Sheila), couldn't avoid hearing the outboard bound train on its daily runs to the cotton gin maybe a quarter mile away. The folks in the dingy white church just up the road no doubt enjoyed having their religious activities interrupted as well.

I grabbed a small suitcase with a couple of changes of clothes and a pair of shoes and trudged up the paved sidewalk past a thigh-high wire fence. Entering the home, I was greeted with a handshake and hug by Lou's dad. I had no idea what the fence was supposed to keep out. Maybe it was designed to keep critters like possum and raccoon from scrounging through the trash containers at the rear of the house, where, taking up part of the rear porch, was a knee-high freezer and a shed with an assortment of contents. I later discovered nothing of value in that old shack. So, I didn't know why any of us were there. Lou never said. Neither did my father.

I had no anticipation about what to expect, as Lou informed no one of her intentions. I knew nothing about the town or the old man's home.

Nevertheless, I was happy to walk inside. Trapped in the 1950s, the living room contained a couch and two padded sofas that faced a small brown, plastic-trimmed RCA Victor television set. The home also had three bedrooms – one was in the attic – a kitchen, and a bathroom with a show-erless tub, sink, moderate-sized mirror, and toilet. Patterned wall coverings matched the linoleum on the floors.

To me, it was ideal. Even better, the house was equipped with two hunting dogs, Spike and Speedy. In their outdoor kennels fenced with wire, located behind the shed, they were left undisturbed except when chow time arrived. Grampap let me feed them. They sniffed me as I fed them hard dog food with some bacon scraps the next morning, and they didn't mind being petted. Their tails wagged when greeting me. I now loved Parma just for the dogs. Then again, I was delighted to have escaped the windowless basement that had been my room for seven years.

To have access to a real porch made me smile. Placed on the front porch, stretching three-quarters of the way from one side of the house to the other, was a weathered, yet well-kept, chained swing, and to the side of it, a springy, light blue metal seat near the end of the doorway.

Dad's car sat parked at the front of the house on Railroad Street alongside the fence with a low gate and a short, paved sidewalk that led into the dwelling. A set of railroad tracks set about forty feet from the opposite edge of the road led to the town's cotton gin down the tracks. On the other side of the tracks and up a brief, slight slope was a white church, the one I noticed the first day.

I was assigned to the attic bedroom in which were two family-sized beds, with ample space to fit six kids. With only five kids in the house, there was room enough to spare. Five of us slept in the attic the first night–Diana, Doug, Denny, Helen's six-year-old daughter Sheila, and I. The unexpected arrival of child guests brought excitement to Sheila. She enjoyed kidding around, playing hand slap games, and rock, scissors, paper.

"You kids better settle down, or I'll give you good reason to be quiet," yelled Helen up the staircase to the attic, a challenging distance to walk for the older set. That demand took little pondering as I was dead tired. All pillows and spreads were down-filled, adding a special comfort to my rest.

I awoke the next morning to the sound of "Breakfast!" and rushed downstairs in hopes of beating everyone to the best seat. I sat next to Grampap as the others were yawning their way to the table. Only the women and girls wore bedtime attire. The boys leaped out of bed in the shorts they kept on and slept in, throughout the night.

It was Saturday. Helen created over-easy eggs, hash browns, bacon, coffee, and biscuits with butter and sorghum molasses. No breakfast was complete without a jar of sorghum molasses on the table for Grampap, who combined real soft butter mixed to form a delicious spread. His coffee he refused to drink from a cup. Once stirred and cooled slightly, he poured a portion of the coffee into his mouth with a saucer. I had never seen anyone drink coffee in such a way.

"Why do you drink your coffee from a saucer?" I asked. I heard a slight slurp when he took a sip, and I remarked that if it were me, I'd have the coffee running down my shirt.

"Ah, it's something I learned in the war," he said. "There were often not enough cups to go around wherever we stopped. Men lost the cups they carried, so a saucer was used. It cooled the coffee faster, and any spilling we cared little about 'cause it was all part of the scene. We already looked messy, so why worry?" He also liked to smash the over-easy eggs until they liquefied, and he scooped a bite onto a piece of toast to eat it. "Well, I guess it's time I get to sorting through those generators."

Helen convinced Grampap to wait until the company parted. The generators were stacked in the scrap yard to the right of the house. Inside each one was a good bit of copper that, once removed, made part of his income.

"They're leaving so soon?" asked Grampap.

Lou told him that she and Dad (Bill) "talked about it last night and decided it best we head south. There's work in Tampa, some kind of bridge building he can get on." I thought I, too, was included in the move, but Dad had other plans. "Lou's dad wants you to live with him," he said. "It'll do you some good, and maybe you'll put on some weight. You're a bag of bones. We're leaving tomorrow, so say your goodbyes to your brothers and sister between now and then."

I wasn't sure how to react, so reluctant I was to be alone without my siblings. In all my twelve years, I'd done nothing without them.

Dad's car ran well throughout the trip from Monaca (Sylvan Crest), Pennsylvania to Missouri. While in Parma, he used Lou's beat-up Rambler to help defray the costs of a second-hand eight-by-thirty-seven-foot trailer which he planned on towing to Florida. Before that purchase, I'd heard nothing to indicate leaving Parma was in the plans.

At first, I didn't know what to think about Dad's decision to leave me behind other than the welcome rescue it would bring from the endless hell my parents embraced.

"Will you be back?" I asked, realizing the affection I had for my siblings was about to be transported out of my life. Those terrible conditions I no longer had to experience while they were left to bear it. They had no choice but to endure endless brawls. It felt as though I was abandoning them. I appreciated our childlike devotion to one another, an attachment I would miss. Our shivering, huddled conferences were our means of survival while the fighting went on.

With breakfast over, whatever possessions we owned were taken into the house or carted to the car. The trailer would be hitched to it at the vehicle lot.

"Don't worry about things," Helen said to me. She was in her thirties, a good homemaker and mother, and a seamstress for a clothing company in Malden. "You'll do fine here. You're special to Pa because he has always wanted a second chance to care for a son. Things didn't go well in years past."

"What happened?" I asked. My eyes caught the reaction of my twin brother, who hated the notion of going on without me. Both of us were twelve years of age and considered ourselves inseparable. This would test our single-mindedness. Would it be hard for either of us?

"Your Grampap used to drink a lot," Helen said. "It made him mean and nasty. Once he gave it up, it was too late. His boys were out of the house, living on their own." She gave me a hug and kissed my forehead. The comfort helped build in me a sense of belonging. A boy my age needed the strength of a caring adult.

"You're exactly what he needs to show a boy that he has love to give. All the apologies he's made over the years weren't enough to bind him to his boys, not as close as he liked. You're an answer to prayer." It was the first time I heard words that gave God His rightful place. Too often, it was goddamn this and goddamn that. At Grampap's, I knew things would be different.

Not much was uttered as Dad and the rest of the family drove off, leaving me behind. I walked to the scrapyard located to the right of the house to ask Grampap if he could use some help. "You ought to talk to your Aunt Helen about getting you more clothes, son. What you have on, looks good enough for school. Maybe she knows of a thrift store that sells your small frame size. Get something to work in."

I talked to Aunt Helen about what Grampap mentioned. She heard that one of the Baptist churches took in families' overstocked clothes and sold them cheaply to folks with little money. "Hop in the car. We'll head over to Mount Calvary." The small-town dwellings we passed as we drove the streets looked as though any one of them could be a thrift store.

The drive didn't take long, just up the road to Locust Street. Some sorting was taking place when we got there. I ran for the pants, tried on a few pairs, and asked about coveralls like Grampap wore. I, by now, wanted to be like him.

"Sorry, I believe you're a little small for what we have here at this time," said a nice lady who helped me search. Soon, two pants my size were uncovered in a heap on the table to the rear of the business. When we left, I had in hand two pairs of pants and a couple of shirts – one set for scrap metal work and the other for school. The socks we bought at the five and dime.

My first week at Grampap's went smoothly. Not a single cuss word or loud demand was made. The day held an unaccustomed-to schedule, including breakfast, lunch, and dinner.

Grampap asked me if I'd like to take a drive to see the outer parts of the town. Going to the church and the downtown store was all I'd seen. Now I saw there was a little more, including one gas station, a barber shop, thrift, feed, and an IGA grocery store.

Surrounding the town were cotton fields as far as the eye could see, each one separated by a quarter-acre stretch of woods. At the front of the cotton fields were ditches, about four feet to the top of the water and five feet deep. "That's where I'll be taking you frog gigging," said Grampap. "You'll like that." Reeds jutted through the water, reaching nearly to the top of the ditches.

We didn't go much farther than a mile or two outside the house. He pointed out the school where I would be enrolling the next day. It was a mere three blocks from his house and looked exactly like what a small-town school should be, with no school team displayed or label on the premises. "See you get over there first thing in the morning. If there's paperwork I need to sign, give it to Helen. She's got more experience with schools and the like, seeing as she has Sheila."

My mind reminded me I would be the only Brayshaw in this school. I was sure I'd feel odd. "I've always had my twin brother, Denny, nearby. I guess it's time for me to learn to be alone," I said. Grampap nodded to reaffirm my remark. Being surrounded by a school load of farm kids was okay with me. A few of them wanted to act tough at times, though most of their behaviors were accepting.

"You're not alone, son," Grampap said. "You always have us. We're here for you and will stand with you when you need help with anything. I might not know a whole lot about all these subjects, but Helen might. We'll help you get through no matter what it is."

"Thanks, Grampap." I knew I could trust him, and I felt safe knowing he was on my side.

The skies began to darken. Rain was about to hit. Grampap said, "We best get back to the house. I should cover that potbelly stove that got dropped off about a week ago. I'm figuring it can bring in a good price. It's old but well kept."

"Maybe we ought to make some room for it in the back shed," I said.

"Yea, it may be best kept out of the weather."

It just began to sprinkle when we drove up to the yard. Grampap asked me to retrieve a dolly from the house shed. The rain held back a little as I hurried to get it. We leaned the stove to the front and placed the dolly platform under the rear. I kept it steady while we rolled it into the rear scrap shed. Luckily, the last purchase of items from that guy from Sikeston left ample room for the stove. I liked it a lot and thought maybe one day we could find some use for it.

This was Saturday. On weekdays, Helen normally arrived home from work around 4:30 p.m. Throughout the week, she rose early to fix breakfast for us and tossed in a load of laundry before laying back down. She worked as a seamstress sewing various things from drapes to clothes, she explained, when we first began to get acquainted. That's when I asked her what had happened to her mother. "Cancer got her some years back." She said that a lot of time had passed, and still, Grampap found it difficult to forgive himself for drinking.

"Your Grampap came home totally smashed one evening," Helen told me. "He shot a rat he spotted hiding near some scrap metal, carried it into the house, and forced my mother to cook it for him."

"Yuck, how gross! She cooked it?"

"Yep, just like she did any other critter Pa brought home from hunting."

"And he ate it?"

"Every bite. But that was the last time he ever pulled a stunt like that because Ma was ready to leave him. She threatened to. Pa felt so sorry that he repented the next morning and swore off booze forever. He's never had a drink since." No drop of drink was noticeable in the house either, unless Grampap kept some for medicinal or hunting purposes.

It didn't take a seer to perceive the gentle, kind character of Grampap. He was, for me, a godsend. His lifestyle was like a dream come true, and his home quickly became my favorite place in the world.

Much like a typical television version of an aged patriarch, he seemed. A lump of tobacco in his mouth he spit into a large empty can of Maxwell House coffee, wore blue bibbed OshKosh B'gosh coveralls with an engineer's cap, and listened when I spoke. Wearing a fisherman's cap while in the sun was his standard attire for outdoor protection. I, too, was instructed to keep a ball cap on while I was in the sun. His demands, I didn't mind. In fact, his tender instructions made me feel loved and cared for.

He liked using the pronoun "son" when speaking to me, which made me feel truly special. The love I heard in that word fought off all the many times I was assaulted by what my father likened me to–a hopeless kid with no fighting skills. "You wait till the Navy gets you. They'll make a man out of you!" he used to tell me.

To him, it was the biggest hurdle of a boy's life to survive military enlistment. It was by those dares to join the Navy that a few years later, I fled from our unstable home to enlist. Next on my list was my deep desire for an academic career, both of which eventually came to pass.

The administrators at Parma's Junior High School were well impressed by my achievements. In fact, I was thought to be an exceptional student whose accomplishments exceeded that of any student in the school. By Grampap's example, being a man who handled difficulties sanely, compassionately, and without emotional outbursts, my former life began to fade far from memory. There never arose a sense of criminal urgency while residing in Parma.

Instead, I lived in an atmosphere of love. At times, I often felt sorry for my siblings and prayed with all my heart that God would deliver them out of the mouth of the lion, which He failed to do in good time. I supposed some people were meant to endure more suffering than others. Don't ask me why they were. I have no clue, and even after becoming a Christian, I still can't say why.

A few blocks to the Junior high school, I walked every day. The educational system wasn't like that of Pennsylvania because it was simpler and less filled with walls of athletic metals signifying success either in sports or academics. The classrooms were uncomplicated, built for the simple, primary purpose of training a child in the simplest of life's needs. In history class, we talked about the usual stories taught at a level less than what my former school instructed. In math, we walked in triplets to the chalkboard to work out problems. I enjoyed the open approach as it was more hands-on and gave me an idea of where each student stood. The better I knew the students, the easier it would be to find one to tutor. But the approach was more than that. It was more competitive and stuck to the topic rather than wandering off like the history courses.

The curriculum in Pennsylvania was, without a doubt, a few steps ahead of Parma's. Their teaching data was up to two years behind in content, depending upon the subject, which allowed me to whiz through the courses. That knowledge enabled me to tutor a few students in most subjects, and my fee was nothing more than the price of the day's lunch. So, I was popular, though not as accessible as the students liked, for I ran home after school just to be with Grampap. In fact, I never had even one same-aged friend visit me. The reason came down to my grandfather being all I needed.

Neither did athletics interest me. Sports were too much of a deterrent from my work in the scrapyard and hunting. And besides, I would not find out until decades later that I was born with spinal stenosis from my neck down to my lumbar. It was for the better that I avoided contact sports. At an advanced age, the inner spine compression would plague me.

Grampap encouraged me to put effort into memorizing types of metals. It was key to understanding the business, which I learned fast. Honing knives, sharpening tools, and skinning critters, he also taught me. The quarter-acre lot to the right of the house contained mounds of metal debris with which Grampap 'drilled into me' the scrap metal business. I combed through truckloads of metallic odds and ends purchased from local scrounges to examine with a magnet in hand, pointing out steel, iron, cast iron, copper, brass, aluminum, and lead. The copper, brass, and aluminum brought in the most money. The other worthless debris we practically gave away, as it was cheap and useless; not good for any real money making.

My pockets held nothing like what I carried in Pennsylvania. Rather than a dull red Cub Scout knife, I now held a well-sharpened Oldtimer jackknife in my pocket and a slim, round, four-inch magnet, both indispensable tools for scrap metal work. We cut out lots of unsuspecting parts from bed frames, lamps, antennae, thermometers, generators, bed headers, radiators, and electrical appliances, piling the best of our finds in the moderately-sized shed sitting on the back, right side of the property. Grampap kept those doors locked.

The removal of copper from car and truck generators was a shared job. I held a long chisel onto which was attached a wooden handle that I set against the side of the hollow metal cylinders of each generator. Grampap, standing up, swung a sledgehammer, never missing, onto the top of the chisel head to break the attachments. The copper, coated with a kind of paper-like substance, broke off in large numbers. We set a blistering fire with an accelerant in the center of a rubber tire, and into it we dropped the wrapped copper to melt off the coverings.

To make quality fishing sinkers, we poured melted lead into molds. Ironically, neither of us found our way to a fishing hole, as we were more attached to possum hunting, no matter the weather, with Spike and Speedy, two treeing walker coon hounds, yelping as they led the way. The overstock of sinkers we sold to bait and tackle shops in the more prosperous towns. The proprietors always sold them shortly after receiving our stock.

"Say, Frank, you pour me a hundred spoon and teardrop sinkers for the next time you come to Millie's; I'd be much obliged," said one proprietor. "Ozark has plenty of buyers. You're a good contact. I'll make it worth your effort." And so, we poured as many sinkers as the quantity of lead allowed.

Grampap's backyard was small, with sufficient space to fit a sizable shed and two dog kennels, occupied by Spike on the left and Speedy on the right. I looked forward to possum hunting on weekend evenings. To us, the hunt was called both possum and/or coon hunting since we shot and ate both animals–tasty dishes in Helen's hands. We used dogs in hunting wildlife in Missouri except for killing bear, deer, elk, turkey, muskrat, mink, river otter, and beaver. No one I knew coon hunted without a dog. That seemed improbable to me. Hunter orange attire was required, but many nights we hunted in our everyday attire. Our pocketed jackets were stuffed with shells and batteries. Grampap used his twenty-gauge shotgun for ending the lives of our next meals.

On Friday evenings, Grampap and I prepared the truck for the late evening hunt. The bed, meant to hold Spike and Speedy, demanded the removal of unnecessary debris. I swept the floor as clean as possible, always fearing some piece of stuck metal would jab into one of the hounds. I attached leather side ties to my belt, as I was the carrier of the kills. I tied those straps to the dead possums' legs, then readied another length of the strap for the next kill.

If the dogs lost the scent of a coon or possum, they sometimes followed an unwanted critter, such as a bobcat, which happened one night. Grampap must have shot that bobcat six times, trying to get his dead body out of the tall fork of a tree. He knew if it remained there, it could cause a dog to misdirect his scent, and besides, the pelt might have been a valuable one if he got it down without shredding it. Hides have various uses for hunters.

"You want a shot at him, son? Just lift the gun to your shoulder, take aim at the bobcat with the bead at the end of the barrel, and let him have it." A couple of shots later, he was still there, stuck in the tree as if he'd been stapled to the trunk. After that, it was a wasted hunt because the dogs would remain on a bobcat scent the remainder of the night, and we wanted possum or coon, except for the pelt of a bobcat, if it was kept intact. This one was shot to pieces.

Pelts from small animals, like possums and raccoons, make ideal fur liners for coats, fur collars, and scarves, and some hometown ladies sewed them into warm possum-fur blankets. Plucked possum furs need to be spun with sheep's wool to create soft and luxurious sweaters, hats, and scarves. Possum-leather products are virtually indestructible.

How Grampap cleaned our kill caught my interest. To me, it became a symbol of adulthood to skin a coon. "If I could learn to do that, it would be my rise to manhood," I thought to myself.

"Can I watch you clean the possum, Grampa?" I asked with great curiosity.

He nailed the tip of the critter's nose to the side of the shed. "Sure, son, come over here." He held a hammer in one hand and a nail in the other. Funny how a carpenter's tool could add to a successful hunt.

He told me he did not plan to sell the hide so that he would remove the head in the end. "A fur buyer isn't interested in the tail, so that will be removed, but the fur around the head they prefer." A long knife with a sharpened blade and a medium-handled hatchet he used, to quickly get the job done.

Had he wanted to sell the pelt, he would have removed it from around the ears and eyes. That would start the cleaning hanging from the tail down.

Instead, he nailed the nose to the shed, not caring about the pelt on the head, and began cutting around the paws, tail, and head, then pulled down on the hide to remove the pelt from the body.

"You see, you work the pelt free around the neck, pulling down, using your knife, if you need help to free it. Stay close to the meat without cutting into it as you pull down. See here, how the legs are pulling free?"

The removal of the pelt went smoothly. I stood surprised by how it practically slid apart from the body.

"My penknife would likely cut as well, aye, Grampap?"

"No doubt. I've tested your work. You hone a knife well. You want a try at it?"

"Sure, what'll I do?"

"Just stick your knife into his gut but not too far, just far enough into him to allow his insides to slide out. There you go, now slide up the knife edge to his throat and open him wide. Now pull out the guts. You got it. Don't be afraid of the blood; all critters have blood. Just pull it out like it's nothing more than chicken gizzards and livers like your Aunt Helen does when she fixes a turkey. That's it. Now let it fall to the ground. I'll deal with the pelt."

I got a kick out of how rapidly the skinning got done and was amazed by how much meat clung to the possum. The pelt was left hanging on the shed to dry. We ate a couple of possums in a meal that would have tasted gamey had Aunt Helen not marinated the meat as well as she did. She could make any kill taste good.

One night, while hunting, we lost the sound of Speedy. Spike came back to the truck, but Speedy didn't appear for hours. Grampap, Spike, and I drove home and returned the next morning to search for him. I prayed he wasn't hurt. After reaching the woods we'd walked the night before, we found Speedy tangled painfully in barbed wire, which we cut, then carried him carefully into the bed of the truck. The vet said there wasn't more he could do but stitch his wounds and to let nature take its course. There wasn't a day I didn't check on Speedy to see how the stitches were holding up. I'd scratch him under his right ear, and he'd bend in that direction to say thanks. No doubt in my mind there was real, palpable love there.

Parma held slightly over a thousand residents in 1965. Small-town life suited me just fine as a boy because I adored everything about the lifestyle. Composed of flat land, the area had not a hill in sight. Cotton fields saturated the scenery in every direction. Separating one field from another were patches of woods of various sizes into which we hiked on our Friday nights hunting.

Today, consolidation has eliminated the use of a hometown high school. Has that helped? I don't know. In the years prior to the automation of the cotton industry, a portion of the kids planned to work within the business, which may have been the reason for the lower academic curriculum.

Grampap was proud of my grades on my report card during the early 60s, but that didn't relax my responsibilities at home. I still did my chores, worked in the yard, cut the grass, and swept both the front and back porches.

Helen also gave me chores, like helping with the dishes and taking out the trash. She worked as a seamstress for a company ten miles from the house, and her excellent cooking was just what I needed as an active, hard-working boy. Everything Grampap and I brought home, including opossum, squirrel, dove, duck, and other fowl, got marinated in a liquid blend of spices overnight and cooked to perfection for the next evening meal.

An exceptional housekeeper, Helen was a good pick for a man in search of a well-run home. She maintained a house well and demanded scrapyard grime be thoroughly washed off my hands before sitting at the table.

As much as I could tell, she didn't date during the time I lived there, but then, I was too young to notice and too busy with my own boyhood activities. As I previously mentioned, when it came to having friends outside of school, I had none. Not a single kid ever came by the house to ask me to do anything with him. A roller-skating rink existed a few blocks from the house, and on many weekend nights, when we set aside hunting, I'd rent a pair of skates and get on the floor.

I skated well, enough to get around the circle at a moderate pace. However, never did I learn to skate backward or ask a girl to skate with me. I felt too inexperienced and feared I'd cause us to crash.

One night I talked to the proprietor's seventeen-year-old daughter. Being a bit underage, she didn't seem to mind that I was only twelve. She tutored kids at school too. "You guys must make a pretty good living with this rink, Cathy," I said.

"Dad says it's a big headache most of the time because there's always something that needs to be repaired and cleaned. Upkeep is constant. He's talked about selling it." It was a clean establishment, though once I discovered the demands, it did appear to be a good bit of work, even for a family with kids that helped.

"I'd hate to see this place handed over to someone else. Your family does a great job, and we know you, all of us here in Parma," I said, noticing just how pretty Cathy was.

"That's easy for you to think. There's insurance and licenses and repairs on things people break, like the candy machine. Some kid kicked it hard or used a pipe when what he wanted didn't come out. That had to be replaced, and then there's the cleaning. You'd be surprised what kids drop on the floor and roll over. Dad's still paying off the hardwood flooring. Now, we hear concrete floors are being poured in the newer rinks. It allows for more spin-ning and power moves. Maybe the insurance is more expensive for concrete; I don't know."

"The music is a great hit with me. It's never too loud, and I know the words to lots of the country songs. Grampap and I listen to western music every Saturday."

"There's another cost," Cathy added. "Some group, what's their name? ASCAP, yeah, they're forcing Dad to pay for using copyrighted music. We're just a small town and serve mostly underpaid residents. Who do they think we are? This isn't a big city. I guess that's why I plan to leave here as soon as I can. Maybe join the military. I need more options."

"Wow, I never thought about all that. I have always known I would someday join the Navy. My Dad enlisted in the Navy, in the submarine corp." It was to partly prove to him, when I joined, that I really was a man, although he refused to speak to me as an equal for most of my life. I was always, to him, some slow boy with little street smarts.

"Listen, it was nice to talk to you, Dave, but I better get over to the front room. Folks want to check out." After leaving, I reached home in no time.

Grampap's children, he felt, could have been better fathered had he not been an alcoholic in years past. I represented his second chance, a do-over. With his drinking far behind him, the best of him emerged. We were close buddies because of his loving chastisement as a substitute father and the fair play of a friend. Folks in town noticed how my addition to the Catron home changed Grampap's grumbly mood to a happier, more enthusiastic attitude. He loved life and loved the purpose it gave him to plan his life around me.

In addition to skating, when not hunting on weekend nights, Grampap and I would go gigging for frogs that lived in the ditches at the front of the cotton fields. Frog legs were one of the most satisfying foods I'd ever eaten. I understand few of those ditches still exist after being filled in with dirt decades ago to provide safer and simpler entry by modernized machinery into the fields. When I first heard of the loss of the ditches, it made me miss our nights of gigging even more. None of those associated with that decision must have been frog leg eaters.

The few that remain have a couple of problems that frustrate the gigging: large mosquito infestations bite giggers without ceasing, poisonous water moccasins have increased in number, and the frogs now turn their backs to the lights pointed at them. There's no way to paralyze them as in times past.

Sadly, no plans to construct new habitats for frogs are in the plans. Their numbers once numbered in the multi-hundreds or more.

A night of frog gigging would start with a flat-bottomed boat constructed of aluminum with two seats, usually bench-type, being lifted into the bed of the truck. Once at a favorite spot, we pulled off the jon boat and laid it on the ground, lit our carbide headlamps, maneuvered the boat into the water, walked down the slope, then sat in the boat as it floated on a water-filled ditch.

The brightness of both our headlamps and a brilliant flashlight caused the frogs to paralyze with fear, which allowed the gig holder to sneak his pointed weapon up to the critter and stab him through. On average, about twenty frogs were killed in a night. Jabbing frogs with a gig was as much a part of our food roundups as hunting possum. It was a positive population control measure. And in addition, frog legs are a gourmet treat.

Saturday was our day of sitting on the porch sipping on sodas, viewing country music shows on TV, and hunting possum. Grampap would smoke a cigar while outside and refused to drink any sort of alcoholic beverage. I loved that about him. At twelve, I'd seen enough of boozing to last a lifetime.

Grampap drank in years past, just like most of his family and grandchildren continued to do. His son, Frank, was the heaviest drinker I'd ever met. Years later, after my naval discharge, I saw Frank's drinking habit firsthand. We were working on the Gandy Bridge in Tampa and rode to work together. Every morning and every day after work, he'd buy a fifth of Old Crow from a liquor store on our route to and from work.

During our Saturday rest, while we sat on the front porch, Grampap would light a cigar. At other times, he would chew pieces of a cigar or any form of tobacco he had on hand.

One Saturday, when Grampap lit his cigar, I asked him, "Grampap, can I have a puff?" He shook his head and gave a disapproving look. After more pleading, he let me try.

It was a large souvenir cigar bought for him at an airport gift shop. When I put it in my mouth, I had to make quite an effort to smoke. He instructed, "No, son, breathe in through your mouth. Make the tip glow."

I managed a few drags, started getting wheezy, then handed it back to him. "No, it's all yours," he insisted. "You have the rest." But it was no use. I handed it back. I was trying to feel grown up and quickly learned I hated smoking and never again inhaled tobacco smoke.

He knew exactly what was ahead, for as I arose to walk into the house, I threw up all over Aunt Helen's newly laundered wash. Grampap laughed and laughed as I cleaned myself off and fled to my upstairs bedroom to lie down. Helen didn't think it was all that funny and scolded Grampap for his mean playfulness. He'd wanted to teach me a lesson.

Grampap bought tobacco in several forms. None of them escaped his appetite. They included tobacco shredded in a sack, shaped as a twist, and powder-like as with snuff.

One night, near dawn, I could hear Grampap coughing and gagging loudly downstairs. I ran from my bedroom to see what was happening.

"Get back to bed," Helen instructed. "It's just your grandfather gagging on his tobacco." At bedtime, he had left a plug in his mouth and accidentally swallowed it.

I tried chewing, but if I had anything in my mouth, it was impossible to halt the natural impulse to swallow. But not for Grampap. He could last a night in bed with a chaw in his mouth and never swallow the first drop but would instead spit it out into a metal coffee can, one of several he placed around the house.

I walked up the stairs to my room that night, refusing to let myself fall asleep until I knew Grampap had safely passed out before me.

Also, on Saturdays, after our time on the porch, we'd go inside to watch bluegrass and country bands play on TV. *The Rhodes Show*, *The Porter Wagoner Show* (sometimes with Dolly Parton), *The Grand 'Ole Opry*, and *Flatt and Scruggs* were our favorites. Thirty years later, I'd be singing and playing bass to those tunes in a variety band, in clubs and resorts up and down the Florida Gulf Coast.

CHAPTER 4:

The Unexpected

One day, I came upon a stack of soda bottles while going through the metals shed for something that has, by now, slipped my memory. "Finders keepers, losers weepers," I told myself. I lifted two wooden cases and lugged them downtown to the IGA to redeem them, gaining what today resembles a few pennies, but for a boy in the early 60s, a dollar was a bundle. By the time I reached home, I'd spent most of that money on junk food.

I walked onto the property and spotted Grampap watching me.

"Where've you been, son?" His voice sounded stern as I stepped onto the front porch. I had no clue what I'd done wrong. Those next seconds lasted an eternity.

"I got a call from the store manager. He told me what you've been up to," he said. I still had no idea what he was talking about.

He explained he made an agreement with the store owner that allowed him to not pay for the deposit on soda bottles. Returning them to the store in the same condition became payment enough. Grampap said I should have explained to him what I'd found. Presumption led me to do wrong.

"I'm sorry," I said, immediately surrendering the few cents I carried in my pockets.

"Stay at home until I get back," Grampap said.

He left to straighten things out with the grocer. That gave him time to consider what to do regarding my dereliction.

Soon the truck came around the corner. Grampap got out and motioned me to sit near him.

"I believe it would be good for you to go to church on Sunday mornings, over there, at the Baptist Church," he told me. "It's obvious to me I'm not teaching you properly right from wrong. I blame myself for your actions. It's best I let God do the straightening."

These days, when I think about it, I figure Grampap wanted to not lose me to bad behaviors. He'd lost the closeness of his sons and didn't want a repeat of those mistakes. He wanted to do right when it came to instructing me. There would be no blunder as he'd done with his own kids. And what better place could there be to learn to do good than God's house?

I still consider it odd that no one else in the household took part in acquiring ethics training. His love for me was very alive and deeply rooted in his heart. 'He' wanted to do what he felt was best for me. My presence in the church, a well-meaning gesture, was intended to teach what Grampap and Helen assumed they could not convey, an acquaintance with the exact uprightness the Scriptures contained.

I'd never known this sort of love and devotion in all my twelve years. It didn't dawn on me until some years later that my stay at Grampap's house was a kind of catalyst for spiritual training, although, as I recall, the lessons presented to my age group in that church held little depth when it came to introducing me to God. The messages were the feel-good kind which contained less Scripture than moralizing. A restoration of conscience was the teacher's aim, not a personal relationship with Jesus Christ.

I learned, as I started to grow as a believer, the first step for me was to be led into a prayer of repentance. Then, as I noticed in my inspection of the materials, was instruction on the three avenues of training–reading, exhortation, and doctrine (1 Timothy 4:13). But there was only reading, which I began to do more in keeping with satisfying Grampap's expectation of me. The Bible will hold its own messages for me, I concluded, so that's what I did. I read.

Not being the informed Christian I came to be months before my naval discharge, I realized my earlier introduction to the things of God became more of a religious ritual, similar to attending a funeral or wedding. It was merely a ceremony, as there existed little depth in doctrine. Perhaps that was because I was still an adolescent meant to attend church to feel good, nothing more. The rest of our household may not have read the Bible throughout their lives. At least Grampap knew where a foundation could be built.

The words taught me principles that failed to remain with me long term, as my age had not yet grown to understand principles void of in-depth interpretation. My frequent visits were nothing more than paying my dues for redeeming soda bottles. The intention, though well-meaning, introduced me to shallow passages that barely penetrated my heart. Years later, I learned what the Bible truly held within its pages. That would take another seven years. Grampap sent me to the right place, but the experience limited me regarding the depth of understanding.

One morning, I walked into the house after services when Helen gazed at me and said, "You ought to look better when you go to church. Once you finish your chores tomorrow, come see me. I'll give you the money to get your haircut."

"Yes, ma'am," I replied. "I won't forget." I guess I was looking a bit disheveled, but what scrap metal worker needed to look good? The work was dirty labor, not a fashion show.

Near noon the next day, Helen gave me the two dollars it cost for the haircut. A dime, she added for a treat.

I walked downtown, entered the barbershop, sat in a chair, and waited my turn. With little to say, I listened to a couple of old fellows debating the local news.

"The cotton crop might suffer this year," said one man. "We've had less and less rain, and for what reason? I don't have a clue." His buddy sat nodding.

"Your turn, Dave," the barber, John Young, said. I always liked Mr. Young. He was as much my friend as he was my barber.

"How's things in school?" he asked. He knew I was an excellent student because one of his patrons spoke of me to him. Since then, that was his primary thought of me. He enjoyed pointing me out to his buddies.

"Straight A's," I told him, which made Mr. Young smile. The two men got a kick out of hearing about my accomplishment. One asked me what I wanted to do when I grew older.

"To work the scrap yard. Take over after Grampap retires," I said as I adjusted my seat in the chair.

Mr. Young was half done with me when a tall, loud man threw open the door.

"Did you hear?" he asked. His temperament displayed an over-excitement, as though he had news that would shake the earth.

"No, what's up, Buck?" asked one patron, speculating the news to come would be that the town's one police officer uncovered a crime.

The room quieted.

"Old man Catron died!" he replied. "I saw a bunch of folks at his place. Out front, I noticed a new truck and cars, so I drove by, parked near the scrap yard, and asked what was going on. That old junk dealer's dead. Died taking a nap, they said."

Mr. Young understood Grampap was a father to me and tried to shut up the tattler. It was only gossip to him, but it was my heart he was tearing apart.

Hoping to quiet him, Mr. Young whispered, "This here's Frank's son." He pointed at me with his scissors in hand.

I jumped off the barber chair and ran fast to get home. Several relatives filled the house with their presence by the time I arrived. Uncle Frank's son, Jimmy, took me aside and led me away from the gathering. We walked toward the old cemetery, an eighth of a mile over the tracks, past the roller-skating rink, and sat on a level cement platform to talk.

"Things like this are the hardest times in life," Jimmy told me. "You're gonna hurt for a while, but it will pass in time. I see you go to church, and you believe in God, so you'll get to see your Grampap again one day in heaven. And you know where to learn. With all your strength, press into God's strength. He'll pull you through this. I know your Grampap was your closest friend, we all know that, but he's not gone, not totally, because he's still in your heart, still in your thoughts, and in heaven, where you'll get to see him again." A rock lying on the ground he picked up and threw at a can, a good distance from us. He hit it on the first try.

The services that followed Grampap's passing are a complete blur to me. It was only the pain I felt, as well as the fear of realizing I had no choice but to return to the hell that could never match the love I was leaving.

The life led by my step-relatives who knew best the small-town life, or should I name it the smallest town life, existed in a world that, for most people, can only be imagined. Most folks in those settings liked to keep liquor around for more than simply medicinal reasons. In fact, Uncle Frank drank Old Crow until it killed him at age 55. It was the right time for him to go, some would say, because he was looking at criminal charges of murder when his cirrhosis of the liver kicked in big time while he was out on bail awaiting his trial.

A black man and Frank were out cutting firewood one afternoon, and after tiring, walked back to Frank's front porch, sat in chairs and began their old habit of guzzling down some whiskey. An argument ensued when the fellow wood cutter threatened to take Frank's life. Acting like he wanted to allow the situation to cool off, Frank walked into his house, grabbed his 12-gauge Winchester, returned to the porch, and shot the man.

Frank then walked uptown to the grocery store where his wife, Doris, was working and explained to her the circumstances.

"Mom went in and called the cops," said the only living relative of the family, Dan. "She wasn't too happy, but she was not awfully mad." In minutes, they arrived at the store and arrested Frank, drove him to New Madrid, and booked him.

"That's when Dad got sick," Dan said. "He went to the hospital in Poplar Bluff, and that's where he died."

For a while. Doris remained living in the house on North Railroad Street, where I lived with Grampap as a teen. She bought it, refurbished it a good bit, and left it to her two sons, Dan and Jim. Jim died some three years ago, leaving the house solely to Dan. Rather than moping around, Doris decided to do a bit of traveling and visited friends in South Carolina and Texas.

"She was as okay as she could be under circumstances like that."

Frank was buried "out at the cemetery with Grandma, Grandpa, a great aunt, and two sisters."

I reminded Dan of the times his Dad used to round up his kin in his truck and drive out to pasture land where he'd locate a cow or hog, kill it, and the rest of us would drag the dead creature by the back of the legs and lift it into the back of an International truck.

"All my life, I lived like that," said Dan, "stealing beef and hogs too. A man would need an electric chain hoist to do that work today, and even in those early days, we didn't use one." Today, he prefers to fish and hunt since it would be impossible for one man to undertake the chore of getting a beef critter to the house. "What I need from the store, I buy."

I asked him about that International, which I remember from the old days. "A truck is made to haul, not made for the highway. It's to haul deer out of."

Dan said the scrap yard was sold in 1966 after Aunt Helen inherited the house. "The only thing left there is the house. The bedroom on the left and the back bedroom need new floors. Only Mom's flowers remain."

CHAPTER 5:

El Camino Blanco

I'd had one year of peace before returning to a household of perpetual hostility.

Before Grampap died, my parents and siblings had already enjoyed a donnybrook of swearing and accusations when Dad had bought a trailer, and the car had broken down in Mississippi after an eight-hour drive. Naturally, Lou was drunk. No one knew where she got the alcohol, but it was enough to keep her well-lubricated and fuming for days on end.

Dad got the car into a repair shop and was told the work would take three days. So, Dad asked a series of strangers until finding one willing to hitch up the trailer and pull it to the fellow's property. I can't imagine what the Good Samaritan thought as the profanity erupted around him en route. The entire trip was punctuated with vile criticism that eventually ended with the police paying a visit.

Once the car repairs were complete, my family headed for Tampa, Florida. When they arrived, Dad had seven dollars left in his pocket. He found work as an ironworker and helped to build the northbound part of the Howard Franklin Bridge. The income helped him to park the family trailer in a mobile home park in south Tampa, on El Camino Blanco Boulevard.

That's when Grampap died and Lou flew to Missouri to retrieve me, to lead me 'home.'

In a matter of a year, I had exchanged a settled, loving life with my grandfather for one filled with hunger and terror. Sadly, my father knew all about Lou's destructive behavior but never intervened to defend his children.

When I saw Denny, he shared a story of something that had happened when their car had broken down in Missouri.

Ominously, he told me, "Lou sent me to get a loaf of bread and told me to walk ahead of the trailer into a thick patch of woods. There was a store on the other side of the trees."

I nodded. That store was likely where Lou purchased the booze she had hidden somewhere in the trailer.

Denny continued, "'Just go straight through the trees,' she said."

Denny told me he had complied, and after ten minutes, he got lost in a copse, void of an obvious pathway. He cried and yelled for help as he circled the trees and encountered a hungry, agitated, mean-faced pit bull that stood paralyzed twenty yards away, focused on Denny's moves.

Denny stared at me, wide-eyed and obviously traumatized. "What would you have done? I chose a direction and ran. Scared out of my wits, I knew I was about to be mauled. I ran in one direction and felt petrified, not knowing I was on the right bearing."

He told me ten minutes had passed when he saw a road from a distance and ran for it. He spotted a truck down the road headed toward him. To walk in the middle of the street seemed the right move. He was right. The driver had spotted him. A kind, middle-aged fellow invited Denny to take a seat in his cab. Denny told him his family had ridden in from out of state and that he had gotten lost in search of the store. The man drove Denny to the mart, and Denny bought the bread while the driver waited for him. The gentleman also took him back to the trailer.

Denny told me he'd confronted Lou when he'd returned to that chamber of horrors called a home. "I know you did that, Lou, to kill me, didn't you? You wanted me to get lost or bitten by that dog that you saw. You wanted me dead, didn't you?"

Dad didn't think Lou's advice was intentional, but Denny felt it had all the marks of a setup.

To this day, Denny believes it was Lou's aim to free herself from him in those woods. She hid her criminal mind well when with others, but it often manifested when proving her desire to wipe out the entire family. Again and again, her evil intent came out as threats to kill everyone in their sleep. She must have noticed the mongrel and used Denny as bait.

Dad knew of Lou's evil personality, the immoral thoughts she possessed that led him by the nose, yet he would not let go of her, no matter the expense, no matter how often they cursed, fought, and maintained a lack of sanity. Neither Dad nor Lou realized their own lack of conscience.

What could I have done? I knew zilch about these events. It felt like a whole new world to me, to have lived a settled life. Hunger and terror were the only emotions generated by these two immature, deranged parents.

We didn't stay long in the trailer park on El Camino, which today looks nothing like it did in those days. Now, it is part of Tampa's southern slum. One day, the owner knocked on the door with several policemen accompanying him. He handed over a court order demanding that we relocate. Apparently, neighbors didn't appreciate the extended shouting and accusations that followed Lou returning from the nearby Hitching Post bar after hours, working herself toward inebriation by caging free drinks from any man who stopped by.

Dad's response was to use some of his pay to put a down payment on land a few blocks from the trailer park. On a good day, the residents would probably hear Dad and Lou going at it but would be less willing to do anything about it. Dad actually made a good choice since the quarter-acre lot featured tropical trees and shrubs, a small bit of Florida's natural beauty. He tied up the trailer in the back, away from the road.

At night, when Dad came back from work, he usually had to go to the Hitching Post, grab Lou, and demand that she returns home. She resisted, insisting there was no reason to "go back to those dumb ass bastards you call children."

When we did have dinner together, I learned to duck as Lou took dead aim with food from her plate and pitched it at us and the walls. She didn't stop there but included knives and forks and practically anything she could get her hands on, all the while threatening to cut our throats while we slept. She also kept a .22 handgun, so her threat guaranteed sleepless nights.

One day, Lou emerged from the station wagon with a cold, fierce look on her face. She marched into the trailer and slammed the door so hard that several vertical panes shattered. Dad followed her inside. As we watched, they began to swing wildly at each other.

Lou showed off her limited aim and range by hurling pillows, utensils, dishes, and a portable radio at Dad with limited success. In turn, Dad threw a punch that dented the refrigerator door. Lou promptly picked up a knife in the kitchen, crouched, and lunged toward Dad to stab him. Dad landed a right cross to Lou's face. She collapsed.

Dad then carried her into the back bedroom. An hour later, they were making love.

During the quiet times, with Dad working and Lou keeping her stool warm at the Hitching Post, my siblings and I did our best to maintain the trailer. We were taken to a laundromat. Everything had to be carefully folded and ironed. Lou was never negligent with her own appearance and behavior, and she had strict rules for how bed sheets, towels, wash clothes, underwear, and drapes should look. How ironic when the fights so frequently tore up the trailer.

The El Camino property was about a mile from a bridge that connected Harbour Island and Ybor City. In the summer and on weekends, Denny and I would hitchhike to the bridge to fish for redfish. We caught plenty using dead shrimp as bait. Of course, we cleaned them and put them in the freezer. We also caught stingrays. I'd cut off their stingers and save them in empty pickle jars.

One day, we rented a small rowboat and ventured out onto the bay. Under the hot sun, with a couple of peanut butter and jelly sandwiches for food, we cast our lines. I noticed a large snook floating near the top of the water. It was near the boat and acted lethargic. I could see it moving slowly through the sparkling water, switching its tail almost as an invitation.

I took my snatch hook and slowly reeled toward him. The fish didn't seem concerned. With little effort, I hooked it and pulled it toward the boat. We thought it weighed at least 25 pounds. Not a bit of struggle did it give me. Protests wouldn't have been much help with two active teenagers holding on.

Once onboard, we had to get it home. After tying the boat at the pier, we scrounged around and found an old mop handle and some fishing line. We tied the fish to the pole, hefted it on our shoulders, and began to walk home. There was no point in hitchhiking. We knew no one would pick us up along with that giant fish. Barely weighing one hundred pounds each, we staggered.

We didn't get very far. At one point, we saw Dad drive by, even noticing us, and we yelled for him. He didn't stop. However, the fellow who rented us the boat also had a seafood restaurant. We had maybe gone half a mile, walking on the side of the road like African gunbearers on a safari, but with a fish. The boat owner found us and drove up to two dark-tanned twins whose catch he desperately wanted. By then, we were exhausted. He offered to buy the fish. We had no idea how much to charge and accepted four dollars for what turned out to be a 27-pound snook.

At home, Dad was angry at the price, took the money, and drove us to the restaurant. There, he threw the four dollars at the owner and demanded the return of the fish he "stole" from us. The owner quavered, rightly scared. He had his staff wrap the fish in white paper and divide the pieces into a couple of kitchen bags.

Dad was sure we should have the fish mounted and placed on the wall. We tried to explain that snooks could grow much larger. He didn't know. He'd never fished in his life. Denny and I figured that he wanted the fish more for the food than to hang on the wall. It went into the freezer.

I'll never forget the apprehension that returned as I began again to experience the continuous aggression that absorbed every corner of my life. My face wore the pain of defeat. For the first time in my life, I'd experienced love. I hated the loss. From the highest high to the lowest low, in the length of a Greyhound bus ride to Florida with Lou. I longed to be back with Grampap, to work in the scrap yard, to again be positive and cheerful. If I could survive to graduate high school, I would flee to safety.

CHAPTER 6:

Mill Hunkies and Rednecks

Where I grew up, in four towns within Beaver County, Pennsylvania, there existed a dense blue-collar population. It could not, however, boast of holding the lead in steel production within the US. The replacement of charcoal with coal in the steel-making process revolutionized the industry and tied steelmaking to coal-mining areas, which boosted Pennsylvania's standing in production, but it failed to be in the lead spot. Indiana outproduced the state.

"In the early days," said one former steelworker, "Death in the mill was fucking extreme. Lots of deaths happened in those mills, and men barely lived to be forty." Sitting on his front porch, I walked by, then stopped to talk to a street musician in my days of writing for the Beaver County Times. I thought a feature would be easy to gain from a road player. It wasn't to be.

I guess the retired mill worker noticed me taking notes from that young, talented, but disinterested street guitarist. The homeless guy didn't care, so this elderly fellow and I struck up a conversation. Speaking in a calm tone, he showed dark wrinkles on his face with salt and pepper-colored eyebrows and a hat, which seemed to be his favorite. It sat on his head, suggesting so. Team and company caps, in those days, took the lead in men's low-income apparel.

Our eyes met. "Hi there. What's your name?" I asked. I moved closer.

"Just call me Yeller. I like to be called that. Reminds me of a favorite film." His grin displayed a charm hidden second earlier.

"Isn't that a dog's name, Old Yeller?"

"I worked like a dog all my life. I may as well be called the name of one I always liked."

The calendar was registered in the early 80s. I said it appeared the whole world was changing, with factories closing and families scrounging for an income.

I went back to the mill topic and asked him how the millworkers died, and he said, "It wasn't only the mills that took lives from that damn cruel heat and burns, there were others. Coal mines caved in on men, and gas, too, killed a shitload of them. And then, if they survived, they died from that damn black lung."

"You got any of that?" I asked him. He turned to me as he reached back to better position a small comforter. "Millwork was hot and hard work, son. Don't let ignorance tell you different." He scratched the back of his head and wiped his forehead with his palm.

"Thirsty, huh?" I asked. I wished I had a drink to offer him.

"It's hot today. Luckily, we're not near those ovens. My cousins used to work in factories and mills. I heard them talk more than once about those furnaces."

"If you ask me, these corporate fools know nothing about the dangers of manual labor work. Maybe it is time they closed those hot boxes down for good. Husbands will stay around longer."

Months following, more than 75 percent of the steel-making capacity in the Pittsburgh region shut down. According to Wikipedia, "Once the center of the American steel industry, and still known as 'The Steel City,' today the city of Pittsburgh has no steel mills within its limits, though Pittsburgh-based companies such as US Steel, Ampco Pittsburgh and Allegheny Technologies own several working mills in the Pittsburgh metropolitan area."

I remember, during the happier days of my youth when no one thought the foundries would ever shut down. Oh, they talked of it, and most believed Americans would eventually accept defeat. No doubt, Southwestern Pennsylvania rose to prominence on the back of steel production, but those days had faded.

The men in the foundries called one another "mill hunkies," an ethnic slur that originated in the coal regions of Pennsylvania and West Virginia. Made up of foreign nationals, workers from Slavic, German, Hungarian, Italian, Czech, Polish, and other Eastern European nationalities who went to work in factories, plants, mills, foundries, and various other industrial complexes, they manufactured chemicals, steel, pipe, iron, brass, glass, tin, coal, metal ore, and other non-metallic minerals.

Those massive industrial complexes reached on land, in some cases, to over seven miles in length, as with Jones and Laughlin Steel. The workers built a culture within those borders that included a language steeped in sarcasm and profanity, with a practice of calling nationalities by biased and/or taunting nicknames.

Mill hunky folks resembled the characters in the movie "The Deer Hunter," where men would get off work and head immediately to their favorite fraternal organizations, whether it be the Elks, Moose, American Legion, Polish Falcon Club, VFW, Knights of Columbus or Amvets. They, too, sat at their prospective bars to drink a couple of brews and bullshit with one another before they left for home.

They talked about home projects and the local news and occasionally reminded one another of the battlefields left behind.

A large portion of the fathers in our neighborhood had helped to defeat the Germans and Japanese during the Second World War. In the days prior to my leaving Pennsylvania, over a decade had passed since the end of US involvement in Korea. Determined to keep wartime tradition alive, this country entered into conflict with Vietnam on February 28, 1961.

.I recall the day Dad and I walked into the Legion in time to catch a one-tour pilot reminiscing.

"I took what I figured was the right lead on him, waited until I got close enough, coming in from the side, and opened up with all six guns. Bullets would fly into the cockpits, through and around the engines, and back into the cockpits. Then, when I looked back, I saw no smoke. Did I hit him?" He paused, likely caught up in the past.

"It sounds as if you had blank ammunition," another vet said.

"No, eventually the wing caught flames, and down he went."

I sat spellbound as Dad talked to one of his friends from the back poker table. In my heart, I knew then I would be entering the Navy. Anti-American involvement in the Second World War existed in the 1940s, and marches took place against Vietnam, but not by my consent, not in the 1960s.

The aviator's voice came back. "He started falling, and six huge, long bombs dropped into the water." Startled by those bombs, the former airman said, "I didn't realize the Germans had aircraft big enough to hold that much weaponry." He sipped his beer and announced he had to get home. So proud I felt to be around such a hero.

Oftentimes, millworkers and ironworkers arrived home late for supper, which often angered their wives. My father's favorite place of camaraderie, that very Monaca Legion, gave me a direction to consider.

Foundry work agreed with most of the men. Winters brought the worst times. A worker away from the furnaces felt like an ice cube. Red hot coke in 55-gallon drums kept millworkers warm. Many of them never left the sight.

Mill hunkies earned profitable wages that grew as the years progressed in accordance with their prospective labor unions, which allowed many men to buy a house in the country, one in the mountains, a boat, and a camper. Some men turned their garages into carpentry shops and owned just about every tool in Sears and Ace Hardware.

The mills and foundries each ran on a kind of pecking order. The assortment of positions included supervisor, foreman, and utility laborers. A single group of workers was overseen by a foreman. Larger productions were directed by supervisors. Labor positions included pipe fitters, millwrights, boilermakers, machinists, and welders. Each worker focused on a portion of the production process. Engineers, technicians, and electricians became known as tradesmen.

In no time, the title "mill hunky" would spread to include any worker within a blue-collar community. I knew I didn't want to become a mill worker, despite having been born into the family of a railroad engineer (grandfather) and ironworker (father). In the back of my mind, without giving it a voice, I hungered for a higher level of academia which I could acquire only one way, to enroll in college and dig into the books. But how? I would figure a way.

Mill towns aren't clean. Although the landscape in the summer can be breathtakingly green, everything gets dusted with the soot that gets blown from the stacks by the mills every day. In the winter's snow, black soot fell, and the kids played in it. Remember the beer garden in the movie "The Deer Hunter"? The county where I lived resembled Clairton, the location of that film.

These men knew they had once stood in harm's way for their country and for the mills, and in honor of that, they formed various fraternal organizations where they gathered daily to drink. Most of the men smoked, so bars in those days were filled with the unmistakable smell of cigarettes. Wall colors turned a yellowish shade that no one seemed to notice. Still, all of us kids breathed it in, even the youngest ones, whether at the club or at home.

Dad smoked two packs of Pall Malls daily, while Mom, prior to her passing, smoked four packs of menthols every day. Their cost did not deter, as smokes cost a mere thirty-five cents in the 60s. Emphysema took Dad's life at 77. True for many families. Oxygen tanks became a common sight for men in their 60s and 70s. Men like my Dad went quickest because they welded for a living. Smoke and fumes created a way of life for them.

Some guys went into the military rather than the mill, then returned home following their military discharges to work at a labor level, which would, over time, increase their qualifications. But I didn't want it. A blue-collar lifestyle never appealed to me. I didn't drink alcohol, didn't smoke, didn't hunt until later in life, but rather, merely cast a line into the Beaver River located behind our New Brighton home, my last residence prior to enlisting in the Navy.

Part of the reason I wanted to be free of an industrial working-class existence included my hatred for the life I, and my siblings, were forced to live, much like a reflection of country music lyrics. My experience taught me no other choice but to run, to find a place of safety, and to lay up savings for my planned future education. The GI Bill gave me that, although not in the amount one would imagine. When I finally applied for college benefits four years later, what I got in return for my willingness to be placed in harm's way for my country totaled a mere $220 per month. But more about that later.

I opposed merely getting by in school through minimal achievement, but the lack of mature adult leadership continued to assault our home and kept those dreams hidden from me for nearly four years. And besides, advanced education my father did not promote because he understood my life's work would likely be in a mill. That thought lasted up to the age of eleven when our family moved from Pennsylvania to Missouri.

Others, as I did, chose to enlist in the military prior to their graduation year. For my brother and me, enlisting meant breaking away from the various sources of madness. That was all we wanted, to be free. Some patriotic sensitivity, in the late 60s, served to motivate enlistment by victims of dysfunctional families. They had to break away somehow, perhaps by choice of employment with the Peace Corps, Merchant Marines, or as wandering nomads.

One of the favorite "get over" ploys used to take place in fraternal groups like the American Legion. During the dinner/dances, a raffle took place. A club representative sold tickets with numbers on them, then later in the event, a person from the crowd was selected to pull the lucky ticket. Little did the participants who bought the tickets know the winner was known long before the tickets were sold. One person held the container into which the bought tickets were dropped, another person was the one who pointed out the appointed selector of the ticket, and another person on stage declared the auspicious number, all of which was thoroughly rigged. The person who reached into the container had the ticket already in his/her hand; he handed it to the seller, who gave it over to the stage spokesman. Then, a person out in left field yelled, "I won! I won!" The raffles were rigged, all of which Dad collaborated with many times.

Blue-collar communities have for many years been the brunt of comedic material. There is Jeff Foxworthy, the Cable Guy, and even Archie Bunker, who make light of thoughtless observers. Within factories and mills, men, over decades, formed a language of their own, a mix of mockery, satire, sarcasm, strong vulgarity, racism, alcoholism, and brutality – especially against newbies – with views that, for the most part, remained conservative in regard to the military, but very liberal overall with unions. The main reason, union dependence, began to turn against the workers as demands for benefits and wage increases soared, merely to lose the support of the corporations, which led conservatives to run against them.

In Pennsylvania, few of the mill workers continued their education beyond high school, if they even bothered to graduate. Most sons took jobs in the mills that saturated Beaver County. No high school diploma was required to be accepted as a member of a labor union; therefore, many teens, frustrated by academic disciplines, simply joined an association they felt best would fit their individual skills or one whose membership included friends and/or relatives.

Chatter in the mills consisted of a form of humor that regarded human misery as absurd rather than pitiable or that considered human existence as ironic and pointless but somehow comic. Such talk could be heard in the kitchens and family rooms, which could change personalities into egocentric, biased, closed-minded, apathetic, unemotional, and anti-intellectual people, whether they consisted of welders, carpenters, miners, laborers, steel workers, ironworkers, or men from chemical and glass factories. Their friends found their sarcastic attitudes laughable, even hilarious when in one another's company. And they were funny. Even I laughed.

A boy had to be eighteen years of age, and his union member father had to sign for him in case an incident needed to be addressed. Countless teen boys knew they desired university educations, even while parents seldom planned for their childrens' advanced instruction.

The other career option, of course, on everyone's mind encouraged enlistment in the military. Others joined the construction industry into such groups as the carpenters and ironworkers unions. In later years, all these occupations would collapse in a heap of unemployment.

Not at any time while with my father did he suggest a potential future as a college student because he looked down on advanced academics. I did, however, hear him repeat the words, "You wait till the Navy gets you. They'll make a man out of you."

Early on, Dad quit high school when barely sixteen, lied about his age to a preacher who baptized him, and provided him with a certificate which, in those days, served as proof for Navy recruiters to enlist teens at the end of the Second World War. It corresponded to Dad's plan. He wanted his sons to enlist in the service as soon as possible and, in essence, leave the house, to get out on their own, which Denny and I did in May of 1969.

CHAPTER 7:

Dowdell Jr. High School

Dad was barely employed, between ironworker projects, and unable to give us school lunch money, so, on the back side of Dowdell Junior High in Tampa, Florida, Denny and I flipped coins with other students to win enough to eat. Once I realized money lay on the ground and in trash cans disguised as soda bottles, we always had a source for gambling money.

Both of us took our chances of winning penny after penny, then nickels, then dimes. Seventy cents meant we would be eating cafeteria food. Zero change meant we weren't eating at all, which was common. There were two-coin games we played. Either we held the coin under our thumbs and called even or odd, or we tossed coins at a wall to see whose nickel landed the closest to it.

Nickels made the best coins to toss as they allowed better control and could, in some games, lean against the wall, which was a sure win. But then, that's all that was won–all the nickels that were thrown. It was the quarter games that added to the biggest wins. Half-dollar coins, though they existed in those days, were seldom seen in the hands of even the most popular gamblers.

So often, I have remarked over the years that I thought most of the gambling I did as a boy gave my opponent the upper hand no matter the competition. I simply did not know how to cheat, no matter the game. Some years later, in another state, we swapped our coin tossing for poker games held in our home's basement. I knew cheating took place by our so-called friends, but the naivete I possessed kept those secrets from me.

Gambling made me feel a bit like a sucker, and still, I was glued to the practice. Denny also felt that way. In time, those games paid off, giving us the promise of school lunches waiting for us.

On the junior high grounds, a few girls asked how much I needed to win. That was easy—the cost of the meal–thirty-five cents.

It was an ingenious method to collect pop bottles to recover their deposit amounts. The method stuck with me well into my university days. With a second backpack, I picked up glass bottles lying on the roadways as I hitched rides to and from my classes.

Getting around, traveling from place to place, and hitchhiking, held plenty of surprises. Cars pulled over for me with my thumb out as early as grade school. None of it bothered me. Not even when the odds seemed against me.

Lots of different attitudes and characters I encountered while sitting in the cars of strangers. Many times, the drivers propositioned me, asking if they might have sex with me, which I always refused. Then I would immediately demand, "Will you please drop me off at this corner?"

Nothing was forced on me. The men and women who picked me up let me out of their vehicles and drove away just as I asked without harming or threatening me. I was sitting in one fellow's car for a couple of miles when he turned to ask me, "Can I suck......?"

"You will not! Let me out of this car right now!" I insisted.

The request to be let out caused no repercussions, just a sarcastic laugh and words that informed me I was truly missing out. Those days, even as an early teen, I believed in angels.

Being without consistent funds, not even an allowance, I soon stole whatever I needed from stores and tabletops. I suppose I should have considered other ways to earn some cash, but what would that be? Cut grass? Shovel snow? Wash windows? Those thoughts never entered my mind, and besides, we were then living more in Florida than in Pennsylvania. Without the tools I'd need, I had nothing much to offer any homeowner.

I took what I needed for school by shoplifting supplies from stores. It was effortless to carry in with me a used store bag, open it, and place in whatever was needed, including tablets, pens, pencils, erasers, rulers, notebooks, paper clips, whatever was necessary for any class, even gym shorts. There were no video surveillance cameras in those days. All one needed, as Dad would say, was "fast fingers."

"If the damn school wants you two to dress out in gym shorts, then, damn it, they'll furnish them for you," Dad said. I got his message.

That left me with choices to make. Should I steal a pair of shorts from a locker to dress out? Either that or I figured I had to steal from a store. If I chose not to follow the rules, so what? Other kids refused to take part in gym activities. Labeled as "scrounges" by the gym teacher was a group of ten boys who sat in the bleachers while the rest of the class played dodgeball or did flips off a springboard. I fit in with them well until I managed to acquire the required attire. I loved doing flips off the springboard, which was a major incentive for stealing what I needed.

It was while living in our next home in O'Fallon, Missouri that I accomplished most of my pilfering. Attention was impossible as a child of uncaring parents. I was fourteen years old and without anything but my fast fingers to acquire what I needed.

Finally, our family had to leave Tampa for the same reason the six of us left other cities. The ear-splitting screams of our parents caused neighbors to protest. Even though Dad had worked for months to attain an impressive landscape, the police again forced us out of town. The round-the-clock chaos brought the occasional police visits, which twice landed Dad in a cell for a week, so the stacked deck played out.

We four realized what would soon occur. It was anticipated a repeat of the identical sign of deteriorated morality that had haunted us for years. The impending outcome we siblings knew was always sitting on the desk of every Chief of Police, an order to remove the Brayshaws from their home.

"I hate this moving from state to state, Denny, don't you? It's obvious to me there will be no escape from the constant fighting, no matter where this family goes," I said, twiddling a stick through my fingers, looking introspective. I so much wanted a real home, like what I had with Grampap. How I missed our playful activities while on a hunt or working in the scrap yard.

And so, we were shedding another residence.

"First, it was New Brighton, then Parma, then Tampa, to be followed by what—do you know?" I asked my siblings. Each one shook their heads. Again, there would be plenty to miss. The fishing in Tampa was fantastic, and that was pretty much what Denny and I lived for.

"I heard them talking about moving to Missouri," Denny said. This time, Dad's goal was a town south of Saint Louis called O'Fallon where we would live, and he could work welding the Saint Louis Arch.

CHAPTER 8:

O'Fallon, Missouri

In O'Fallon, Dad found a house rental and moved in with what limited possessions we owned. While Lou drank through the day, Dad walked on thin metal strips 630 feet in the air on the St. Louis Arch. It could have been a half-decent start to a new life. But it wasn't to be. Instead, life regressed into another immense disaster.

One Saturday, while Dad was repairing the front screen door with an Exacta knife, Lou walked up to him, grabbed the blade out of his hand, and sliced her forearms.

She immediately fled through the door and screamed to the neighborhood.

Blood decorated the entire scene. This was her newest psychotic plan to create proof of Dad's murderous intent by shedding blood right before she ran outside, screaming at people and passing cars. "He's trying to kill me! Help, someone! Please, he wants me dead!" Neighbors came quickly out of their homes to see if it was one of their loved ones in trouble.

After several minutes, sympathetic folks came to Lou's aid and looked at Dad like he was a monster. Pushing them aside, Dad picked up Lou, forced her inside his car, and rushed her to a hospital. A stranger pointed toward the medical center.

Lou soaked the front of the house in blood, which I cleaned up with a bucket of water that I threw at the mess and wiped down with whatever towels I could gather. I could only imagine what the inside of the car would look like.

"This is the worst thing she's ever done. Where did this evil come from? This must be true insanity," I said. Bent over, I continued to scrub the damp red blood from the entrance and screen door. Bucket after bucket of water Denny brought to me. I poured the used water into the plant beds the farthest from the house. My clothes looked like I'd just cleaned a string of possums. Ruined, I threw them into the trash can located at the rear of the house, then took a shower.

Dad and Lou's fighting had increased again to unbearable levels, reaching the ears of all the neighbors surrounding us. Just as before, the police force grew weary of the calls made to them by distraught residents. Their kids' lives were in peril if the Brayshaws were permitted to stay.

The potential legal matters that were about to arise due to police responses to their domestic disturbances kept Dad's mind full of worry.

On a separate occasion, at the same location, during the afternoon, the four of us had just come home from school to find our rented home a disaster. The windows were in pieces. Upon our entering, Lou fled to the bathroom and locked the door.

Dad soon arrived at the house, parked his car, and walked through the front door.

"We can't get into the bathroom!" Denny said. "Lou's inside. She's locked herself in." We imagined Lou was bleeding to death.

"She has a knife," I told Dad. My fingers stretched out to show the size of the blade.

Standing by the door, Dad could not get a response, so he kicked it in with his muscular legs. Lou was lying in the tub, covered in massive amounts of blood.

"Jesus Christ, there's blood everywhere!" And there was. It decorated the walls, the tub, the toilet, and floor and made the deck slippery.

Dad lifted her, turned, and slipped on the blood covering the floor. Instead of caring for himself, he helped Lou to stand and again went crashing to the floor.

Lou, beyond the doorway, ran straight to the house entrance. Dad arose, walked out of the blood, and looked Denny in the face. "Now, what am I supposed to do? If I go chasing after her, the cops will think I'm trying to kill her."

"Let her be. Get her help, but stop allowing her into our lives," I said. My hands were folded prayer-like as I pleaded.

Dad ripped off his bloody T-shirt, wiped the blood off his skin, and dropped the shirt to the floor. To the kitchen sink, he rushed to wash his body. I picked up his clothes and threw them into the outside trash container.

"Dad, maybe you should call the police," I said. Dad hated that because Lou could fabricate horrible stories in seconds. Still, I insisted while the rest of the kids cleaned the house.

"Jesus Kryst," Dad said and ran after his maniac wife. She left a blood trail on the sidewalk, grass, and roadway. Neighbors spotted Dad chasing after that red-drenched lunatic and called the police.

When the police arrived, they cuffed Dad and placed him in a cell. Lou was taken to a hospital, where authorities admitted her. The police declared the incident a domestic dispute and wrote no charges against Dad. I had expected Lou to lie to the point that serious charges would keep him from returning home, at least longer than one day.

At times, Lou had the ability to be convincing to authorities, but the greatest portion of her charges failed to stick. The law's response of driving off with Dad in their back seat was merely a fleeting formality. All I knew concerning this latest event was that Lou was bleeding, she stunk like a street drunk, and Dad had arrived long after she'd committed her self-afflicted deed.

Diana, throughout our initial stay in O'Fallon, was away picking tobacco in Hartford, Connecticut. She was sent there through a work program provided through Dowdell Junior High School in Tampa. A physical examination was required, which she passed.

Near the end of her work commitment, Mom's mother, Nana Celia, called Diana to provide support, at which time Diana discovered Dad had moved the family to O'Fallon, Missouri. Had Nana not called, Diana would have taken a bus to Tampa and alone tried to figure out her next move.

The lady in charge of the tobacco company drove Diana to the bus station to purchase a ticket for St. Louis; otherwise, she would have taken a seat in the wrong transport back to Tampa. The ticket to St. Louis was free, paid for by the tobacco company after being told of the irresponsibility of Diana's parents.

Near the time of this incident at our home in O'Fallon, Diana was making her way to us. She was on the bus, headed to a godforsaken destination, at the time of Lou's bleeding.

Upon her arrival, Dad took the money Diana earned, all $300, and handed back to her only $50, keeping the rest, with no explanation as to why he refused her the wages she'd earned. She would need school clothes and other necessities, which was the primary purpose of her picking tobacco. Dad allowed her only a small portion.

As habits went, the police came to the house and demanded that Dad remove his family from their town. They insisted that he relocate out of O'Fallon by midnight that very evening to keep the neighborhood safe for passersby and children. This forced Dad to walk away from one of his highest-paying employment positions, welding the steel beams of the St. Louis Arch.

None of us kids knew anything except that we were back on the road without possessions or a destination. What a shame. It could have been a wonderful existence. But it wasn't to be.

To control an intoxicated hillbilly from the backwoods was like carting a distressed, captured bobcat from town to town. Normalcy was not to Lou's liking. She wanted her insane idea of freedom, not responsibility or secure family life. All she cared for was alcohol and her desire for a drinking partner, and when Dad refused, hell always broke loose with threats to end everyone's lives. Even when he gave in, the same occurred. There was no way to win.

Despite all the torment we endured as kids, I still loved my father, who refused to free us from his attachment to that maniac. My love for him, however, was never enough to gracefully accept his chosen lifestyle, especially when it affected his kids. We lived entirely different lives and were, in no way, morally or intellectually alike. We never thought the same, except that we shared in the horrors of our years together.

Even after I had enlisted in the Navy, was discharged, and entered the university, Dad refused to accept me on equal terms. He hated the demands of education, hated any form of authority, and he was convinced the world owed him. At the same time, while in my youngest days, I knew how to get by. I admit I learned that skill from my father. It is one thing he passed on to me that stuck.

As a young boy, my father would lead me into department stores, which, in those days, were much smaller. W.G. Grant was one of them in southwestern Pennsylvania. He'd take me into the boys' section, select a pair of pants my size, grab a shirt, then tell me to put them on, along with a new belt. A pair of shoes he would bring to me in the fitting room where he would smear dirt on them from the pair I'd worn into the store, and we'd walk out of the store together without a care.

He never purchased packaged deli meats or meats of any kind. They all fit nicely inside his shirt or pants. Even with holiday turkeys he would get to the car. Placed inside of boxes, he told the guys in the back room that he needed them because he was moving to a new apartment. While at his trailer in Ohio during the months prior to his death, I opened the refrigerator to get something to eat to find it overflowing with packaged luncheon meats.

Often, Dad would dress in clothes resembling a department store trucker. He'd enter the store pushing a dolly and return to a borrowed truck with a brand-new refrigerator. After placing a large "sold" sign on the appliance, he'd load it into his truck and drive home. This he did to obtain a freezer, a television set, and a top-of-the-line weather radio, just to mention a few items.

Other things he collected from stores were cassette tapes, eight-track tapes, all shaving and cleaning items, socks, candies, and even a child's plastic swimming pool, which he carried out with his old "sold" sign trick.

Dad took things for more reasons than to support his family's needs. He greatly enjoyed the game. But he wasn't always on top of it. On one occasion, when Mom was in the hospital, we were headed for the drive-in to watch 'Lil Abner and Suzi Wong; Dad decided to stop at the W.G. Grant department store to get us some candy.

As he was returning to the car, a clerk came running out of the store's entry, yelling for him to stop.

"I saw you. You stole that candy. You didn't pay for it. Stay here; I'm calling the police." Dad looked at us and told us to think nothing of it. "The guy's out of his mind," he said. I don't recall if he walked off with candy or not, nor if we ate anything while at the drive-in theater. The episode didn't remain in my mind long.

Just how was he to do that, anyway? No one owned cell phones. The clerk would have to go back into the store, which he did, and by that time, we were gone. In those days, there weren't surveillance cameras, so there was no proof of Dad doing anything in any store. He told this fellow to go "scrub his ass" as we drove out of the lot.

Dead for many years now, I can still hear Dad say, "The Good Lord blessed me with quick fingers." Was he ever caught? A couple of times–once, when he took home some tools from a work site. He lent one out to a friend; then, when they had a fight, the guy turned him in. The outcome was a six-month sentence to a work camp filling sandbags, but not for long. He convinced the authorities he had a bad back and that he couldn't do the work, and they released him.

CHAPTER 9:

Grove City

"Where are we headed now?" I asked, tired of our bouncing from place to place. "I heard them considering a house near Columbus," Denny said. "Dad knows the union boss there, an old buddy of his from Pennsylvania." Denny's arms went searching for a map. He found one, but it didn't take in all the states we would be passing through, so it wasn't much help.

I shivered thinking of those terribly cold winters we were about to experience. "When we were younger, I remember Dad driving to Ohio to visit Grandma, but I don't think we ever saw Columbus," I said. "I hear it's a terribly cold town."

"Below freezing some days," Denny said. Cold temperatures we recalled from our young sled riding times at the same latitude in Pennsylvania.

A couple of amusing distractions in this town I yearned for, not simply another temporary school enrollment. Maybe the school would offer extra-curricular activities that suited my skinny frame.

Then, pessimism overwhelmed me. "I figure we'll be in and out of this school in less than six months. You wanna wager?" I added.

Earlier homes proved my theory. Life resembled that of a military brat by the many stops and starts between school semesters we experienced. Talking to the son of a Navy lifer one day, I discovered enrollment in schools for a child could grow to six schools in a year. I think we were closing in on that number.

"Even if there is work from this labor union, those two will keep beating on one another after a few sips of booze. It won't matter. We'll be gone soon enough."

The real reason we left Missouri was no secret. The police threw us out. "Please, Lord, keep us from leaving after a week," I prayed. "This has to be a good place to live."

I liked the residence Dad rented. It had space, a furnished cellar, and a laundry. It would suit a family of six just fine.

That *Hee Haw* country song claimed it best. "Doom, despair, and agony on me, deep dark depression, excessive misery. If it weren't for bad luck, I'd have no luck at all. Doom, despair, and agony on me." It represented our life.

In Grove City, the fighting escalated into a broader dimension of panic and anxiety for us kids. Dad's and Lou's hostility and obscenity exploded, swelled louder and more unrestrained. We kids weren't positive we'd remain alive much longer.

To make matters worse, Lou's sons, Tony and Tom, both our ages, paid us a visit for four to six weeks. They, too, fought like vicious criminals.

I recall one episode, an argument, where they were cursing back and forth, from the upstairs by Tony's room to the basement where Tom stayed. Fed up with Tom's cutting vulgarity, Tony ran to the stairwell of the basement.

Upon reaching the bottom, Tom threw a knife like a professional circus performer. It stuck only a few inches from Tony's head onto a two-by-four. Their favorite line I remember: "You're a dead man. Today is the last day you will draw breath." How close those remarks equaled Lou's threat to murder the five of us.

The negative tone of the house grew beyond imagining because of the lack of calm, now from two parties. When Dad and Lou screamed at one another, they fought and wrestled deadly implements out of each other's hands. Kitchen knives, hammers, and cast-iron pans they used as weapons. Supper seldom got made as the house was again turned into a wreck before any thoughts of a meal emerged.

School bullying brought with it its own difficulties. While walking out of a classroom at the end of the period, I turned after I felt a tap on my shoulder. Twisting my head to see who wanted my attention, instantly a fist struck me in the face, knocking me to the floor. My notes and supplies scattered everywhere around me.

Thinking a fight had begun, the other kids did nothing but stand in a circle to watch. They preferred to observe and refused to break it up. Just as Denny walked by the doorway, I pulled myself up from the floor. He peeked inside to view the commotion and recognized the kid that hit me.

I looked over to Denny. "Denny, you're here! I don't know why...." I struggled to say as Denny's fists started flying.

I learned later that at the start of the day, Denny and this kid had exchanged strong words, and because we looked alike, the kid mistook me for my identical twin brother. I became the target.

Denny rushed in, grabbed the boy, struck him twice in the face, put him in a headlock, and banged the guy's head on the teacher's desk. Next, he slammed him into the chalkboard, then knocked him hard against the chalkboard sill on the bridge of the kid's nose. The fellow was badly torn up.

Both of us earned trips to the principal's office, where the man suspended us from school for ten days. That didn't bother us much because we knew Lou would be out drinking the entire day, which released us to cut up a pile of potatoes, fry a stack of French fries, and watch television.

Dad learned of the incident and seemed proud his sons took care of the problem. We refused to be bullied. By then, I still hadn't learned how to fight well, so bullying would continue to take place against me in the next couple of school years. Not until I entered the Navy did I learn how to better handle myself.

Our time in Grove City introduced Denny and me to the junior high school band. Rather than selecting a musical instrument, in a roundabout way, I tried joining the wrestling team. After many practices, the wrestling coach realized he could not keep me. My small size enabled boys to toss me around like a feather. The school band became my next choice.

After auditioning with a silly country tune on the guitar, Denny was accepted into the jazz band. I followed him after the bandmaster allowed me to study the upright bass to play in the jazz band. But, if I wanted to study the string bass, he insisted I learn to play a marching instrument, as he needed to fill the field with marching players. My instrument turned out to be a xylophone.

I sat in a chair in the practice room as often as I had time. A specially made chair held up the instrument allowing me to wiggle my way close to it to practice. It helped me to study scales, enough so that the teacher declared me to be marching band xylophone player material. My accomplishment on that big brass instrument encouraged the band leader to persuade Denny to also carry a xylophone, whether he could read scores or not. It was the numbers he wanted to add to his group of marchers. We practiced our scales together, and some improvement could be heard in Denny's performance, but it was the guitar to which he was most attached.

Football games we played as scheduled, but after the bass drum player quit, the band leader resorted to me. I never understood why because I could read the xylophone scores and played the instrument well. Unfortunately, I was convinced to set aside that big horn. These days, I think that it was my size that mattered, not my ability. To the crowd, I must have looked like a Holocaust survivor dragging with me a forced burden.

But as I saw it, it didn't matter how small and thin I stood; the bass drum I learned just as well. Percussion sheet music looked awfully odd, and, in time, I learned to understand it, but it really didn't matter as I practically had memorized all the places my drum had to be beaten. I sensed well where a hit on the drum mattered as we marched on the field or sat in the bleachers, so the sheet music really meant little to me over time.

A few of the jazz band members formed a Tijuana band, and together we studied music composed by Herb Alpert. With Denny playing the chord arrangements on his guitar, all of which sounded very passable, I struggled to learn the positions on the school's string bass. As years passed, I saved sufficient funds to purchase my own upright bass and played it in several churches accompanying the keyboardist for various hymns and conventional worship tunes. It was many years before I could perform for church worship services. At this time, I still failed to passably pluck the double bass in jazz band, and anyway, it became time for us to move again at the command of the police department.

Even after several warnings by the Chief of Police, the arguing and vulgarity again grew more and more unbearable for the neighbors. So, we hit the road again, this time back to Pennsylvania. This drive caused me to deeply regret leaving the school band behind, as I was growing to love music above other pastimes.

CHAPTER 10:

New Brighton

A s we drove into Beaver County, Pennsylvania, our ancestral home, after an absence of three and a half years, I expected to see no new landmarks since our departure in 1964. The population decreased primarily as the result of natural population decline, which stemmed from a higher number of deaths than births each year, along with population loss caused by domestic migration. This meant even the oldest homes and businesses built at the turn of the 20th Century continued to be reused for residences and commercial structures. With the population on the decline, there was little call for new houses. Therefore, families continued to buy and sell homes built from 1890 to 1930, which kept up the appearance of the county much the same as when we left it. The imminent doom of the steel industry, which took place in the 80s, had yet to hit.

The one most consistent feature of Southwestern Pennsylvania, the attractive countryside scenery, still captivated me. Healthy and vigorous it appeared when we returned, and to a greater extent years later, when Denny and I returned in 2007 to visit Dad prior to his death on June 25. The bucolic backdrop, in all seasons of the year, consisted of small hills with gentle slopes that extended a long way into the distance with shallow and deep valleys, and cliffs called reliefs, with a height ranging from 200 to 600 feet. There were ridge "lookout" locations where magnificent views spanned across the specific valley, rocky outcrops, and evidence of recurrent landslides.

No roads led by a straight line to a destination, as no straight shot existed anywhere. Drivers in that region had to circle rivers and portions of round, high ground to reach their objective. The flatter lands of Parma surely had their positive side when compared to the winding roads of New Brighton that seem to head nowhere.

Despite the beauty, my interest lay in mere survival within a family steeped in alcoholic addiction and hostility. Denny, Doug, and I shared an upstairs bedroom in a wooden, two-story house that Dad rented on Third Avenue in New Brighton, a town with a population of nearly 8,000 in 1967. Today, that population has decreased to 5,565. It is ironic that in such environmental beauty, a common factor within families in that region–family misery–increased within a space of ten years when aided by unemployment, alcoholism, and the lack of parental responsibility.

Alcohol, in 1964, could only be bought in state stores in Pennsylvania. Today, the state continues to be an alcoholic beverage control state and carries a retail markup of usually 300%. It could be higher for some items and lower for sales items. A four-dollar bottle of wine wholesale sells for sixteen dollars. Spirits are sold only in the state-owned Fine Wine & Good Spirits stores, which also sell wine but not beer. It seems like a rich man's vise, and yet nineteen percent of the state's population suffers from the disease of alcoholism. In contrast, only six percent of the nation's population is afflicted with the disease. This means that twenty percent, or over one thousand people, are alcoholics. In strong support of the habit of alcohol consumption are 545 fraternal organizations in and around Beaver County. Intoxication within these clubs remains extremely popular.

Dad disliked banks and kept his money in cash and hidden in various spots in the house. At least twice, his second wife, Lou, discovered his hideaway, took the cash, and spent every dime on feeding her addiction. What kept those misfits together will forever remain a mystery to me.

The house we occupied in 1967 was built in 1920. Today, our former residence is more conventionally equipped and refurbished with the addition of an outside veranda and rebuilt interior to give it a more updated appearance. I looked at it online on Zillow recently. It is years ahead in refinement, with today's construction materials used for the walls, floors, appliances, doors, windows, and staircase to make it comparatively more elaborate than the likes of our old abode. Years past, the house contained, as it does now, a basement, a backyard with a hill at the far end that deeply slanted onto a sidewalk and brick-layered street not far from the Fallston Bridge. A solid home Dad could have owned for a reasonable price of $10,000 in 1968. He refused the commitment. Today, its value extends beyond $150,000.

If love ever existed between Dad and Lou, it resembled a very crazy sort, born not from above but from far below. Lou's mind could find the harshest words to say to anyone in the family at any time. Any belligerent name in the book, like whore, she used on my sister, who was innocent and only fifteen. She was treated as a slave by Lou, and a victim of Lou's jealousy, for Diana radiated beauty and caught the eye of every boy in town.

Of all the duties forced on Diana, laundry she most hated, which demanded that she drive loads of wash to the laundromat and fold items not to be ironed. The amount to be pressed included nearly every fabric, as well as towels, wash rags, underwear, sheets, pillowcases, tee shirts, socks, drapes, and tablecloths.

Lou continued to do exactly what she'd always done. She would arrive home from one bar after another, sometimes past ten o'clock. If she arrived home near supper hours, she would prepare meals, though they were rushed and not usually appetizing, plus there was no promise the food would remain on separate plates or on the table itself, as she routinely threw it at everyone at the table at the mention of her intoxicated state. As her drunken preparations got underway, Dad would be upstairs to clean himself. But once he came downstairs and noticed her inebriated state, he'd grow angry, and an argument would break out. They would escalate in seconds and eliminate everyone's appetite.

Brawls that took place in the New Brighton house exceeded those in past locations and were the most savage fights I have witnessed. The interminable screams, a constant reminder of the torture we endured for years, we vocally refused to abide. But our pleas went unnoticed.

As they fought upstairs, Dad and Lou tried, at times successfully, to push one another down the staircase that led to the foyer. Not all falls took place because of premeditated plans, but those served to provide Lou with a lie to the police when they arrived. She said Dad physically struck her with various tools. Twice, she accidentally fell down the stairwell due to her drunkenness and claimed Dad broke her ankle, which placed him in a cell for a night. As in years past, Lou continued to sit daily in bars while Denny and I skipped school to practice our guitars and make french fries.

Discussions among our family relatives signified no more than expressions of our messed-up lives. "This life is nothing but a nightmare," Denny would reply. "I wish he'd knock her out for good."

The next time, I'd tell them, "Those are two of the worst people in the world," followed by, "I really believe there is a devil. He lives in their room; I know he does."

Those words, too, were heard by none of our relatives. Neither our uncles, aunts or grandparents involved themselves with our troubles. They had problems of their own.

We kids often asked one another, "Do you think there will be any supper tonight? Maybe we can sneak some peanut butter and a few crackers, do you think?" Diana liked to make herself mayonnaise sandwiches to keep alive.

Dad's favorite adage, "Beans and hot dogs tonight, and hot dogs and beans tomorrow night," intended to teach us kids that life did not always meet expectations. We never knew if there would be a meal to eat or not, no matter the time of day.

And besides, not much could be found in the refrigerator or cupboards to eat for kids who knew so little about how to cook, other than to make french fries and P&J sandwiches. When Lou caught us in the act, we caught hell.

A few neighbors around us had ripened gardens, so we'd sneak, as often as we could, raw corn, radishes, tomatoes, and an occasional melon. One of the owners nearly caught us one night as we ran with our shirts full of stolen vegetables. Fruit trees in the neighborhood served us equally as well. We appreciated the heaps of fresh-grown apples, pears, grapes, cherries, and plums.

As tempers rose higher at home, Diana used to race to a neighbor's home; a family with twelve children. They lived more peacefully than we did but still had rough lives.

While in New Brighton High School, I went to a woodshop class where I constructed a mahogany rifle rack. The finished product looked beautiful. Why I chose a rifle rack remains a mystery to me as I didn't own a rifle or any sort of weapon. I was merely sixteen years old. Once completed, I set off to carry my masterpiece home around my neck. I didn't get very far when a stranger ran out of his house to say he wanted to swap whatever he owned for my rack.

"How about a sled?" he asked. "I have a second one that I no longer need." Nope. "I have a glass chess set that is high quality. I wanted to learn to play but never got around to it. Would you like it?" he continued. Nope. "I know. I own a 20-gauge single-shot shotgun. It's perfect for raccoon, fox, skunk, possum, coyote, bobcat, and weasel at any hour, day or night. Will you take it for the rack?" he pleaded, about to bend to his knees.

His pleas recalled my times on the hunt for possum with my grandfather, and the memories of me with his 20-gauge shotgun. With knowledge of its required maintenance, I took it and made my way home with a dated 20-gauge shotgun that held only one shell. I kept the weapon in the basement of our New Brighton home. In my mind, I knew exactly where I leaned my gun against the wall. I never took it out anywhere to fire that one shot. After a few months, my shotgun became the weapon nearly used to carry out a horrible crime.

One night, Denny stumbled upon my single shot right where I'd left it, against a hidden portion of the basement wall. So fed up with the life he and his siblings hated, he sat in the upstairs hallway in the event Dad's and Lou's bedroom door might open. I only owned one shell, so it would not have been easy to shoot both of them; still, he waited and wondered which one of our lunatic parents would be the first to step out of the bedroom. It would be that person he aimed to kill.

Neither of them had yet come out of the room when Denny fell asleep. Where my shotgun got stored or hidden afterward, I have no idea, and I never got it back. It's likely Dad spotted it and kept it as his own.

As we did in our junior high school days, Denny and I went back to redeeming pop bottles for cash enough to flip coins to eat in the school cafeteria. Many days, we went to school depressed and hungry, with stomachs in a fit.

Despite all the indicators of neglect, not a single relative stepped in to attempt to rescue us children.

"We have our own troubles to contend with," my mother's sister said. And she did, after she left her husband for an old boyfriend for two years, then returned at her children's insistence, soon to follow in their conversion from Catholicism to become Holy Ghost holy rollers, a common nickname for Pentecostals in those days.

And so, we pretended to be a family. Denny and I tried to mitigate the trauma. We took part in basketball games frequently with a few close friends in town, fished below the Fallston Bridge, and learned to play our guitars well enough to perform on theater stages and at state fairs.

"During that time, we played songs like "Sweet Georgia Brown," "Misty," "Five Foot Two," and "Dream," as Denny and I recently recalled while we reminisced about those years.

The millworkers I knew, I could not call uneducated but rather undereducated. Few books held their interest, perhaps the phone book and a Danielle Steele or Louis L'amour novel. People refused to take up study or perusal as a largely popular pastime. My grandfather, a perpetual tinkerer with new home projects, had enjoyed construction endeavors on his property located in Freedom and had grown grapes from which he made wine. Many men took pleasure in their large model railroad stations in their basements with tracks, trees, structures, engineers, trestles, and bridges.

Dad knew well the customs and traditions of the mill culture and reunited with his favorite fraternal organizations to drink and make spirited remarks about wives, women, and family life in general. I discovered this years later, by surprise, when he asked me, after my naval discharge, to tag along with a buddy of his to grab a brew. Without the first bottle drunk, perhaps only three-quarters finished, Dad, out of nowhere, began to vent loudly, negatively, and pointedly vulgar accusations against women in general. That moment, the rest of them harped on about how bitches were not worth the bother to any man, and a woman's aim was the potential destruction of the home. Again, he revealed his warped sense of family.

In the summers, with plants in full bloom, dense and developed, the countryside produced luxuriant greenery wonderful to behold. Industrialization, without apology, had coated landscapes, vehicles, houses, and cultivation with a variety of plants for decades, even, while black soot blew from commercial exhaust stacks. The extraction of mineral resources deep in the soil for raw materials to manufacture iron, steel, glassware, and an assortment of industrialized products was needed to erect skyscrapers, bridges, tunnels, and other construction needs.

The Pennsylvania backdrop in the fall months blanketed the land, vividly multicolored and gorgeous beyond description. The longest walks I took were in Brady's Run Park. The area consisted of 2,000 acres of space that featured a lake, trails, picnic areas, pavilions, a playground, a dog park, and other amenities. To this day, I continue to miss those long walks in that park, the fresh breeze that blew across my body, the sound of the short waterfalls west of the lake, and the refuge the backdrop and sounds provided me while away from home conflicts.

As a middle-aged teen, I fished in many of the small and large streams, creeks, and tributaries that fed into medium and large rivers made up mostly of the Beaver and Ohio rivers. Unfortunately, in those days, the only fish to be caught in the Beaver and Ohio rivers were inedible catfish and large, repulsive carp, both of which I returned to the water or stabbed a few times if one swallowed my hook.

The smallest tributaries carried high levels of sulfur that leached from coal mines and mine waste. My first introduction to sulfur water at a friend's home was an unforgettable experience. The water emitted a repulsive odor and a terribly bitter taste. I barely completed one drink, even a half glass of it. Sulfur water, made from dissolved minerals that contain sulfate, supplied the daily source of water to cook and clean for many family homes, especially those in the country.

Peeking at my life to see what led me to enlist in the military leads one only to a heap of hard times, except for the marvelously short time I had with Grampap. How I wish I could have stayed in Missouri. Now, I again felt neglected, without caring parents and without a vision. Briefly, Grampap's scrap yard held a place for me, but God chose to take him home to Himself, perhaps so I could learn to trust more in Him than in a person.

Because my family had no capital, I entered my teen years without direction. To envision attending a university once I completed my high school education was a dead dream. Mill working parents seldom talked about advanced education, for in them existed little conviction, if any at all, to ignite such a goal for their kids. The community simply learned not to think in those terms.

The mill industry emerged as the primary vision fathers pictured for their children if they predicted anything at all. A few young adults refused the plants, mills, factories, and foundries and chose, rather, to establish shops. There were jewelry stores, dress shops, five and dimes, the start of fast-food chains, welders, auto mechanics, and much more. One of the most successful chains in Southwest Pennsylvania was the Hot Dog Shoppe. We ate there at least twice each week, devouring their chili hot dogs and fries, which all the counties knew was worth a long drive to purchase in New Brighton. We were lucky enough to live near by. We ate there at least twice each week, devouring their chili hot dogs and fries, which all the county knew was worth a long drive to purchase is New Brighton. We were lucky enough to live close by.

As I shared earlier, Pennsylvania's educational requirements challenged me more than the syllabus I'd encountered in Parma. Still, without money, there was no college ahead for me.

Missouri state educators, by their own standards, said I'd attained the level of an exceptional student in their school system. Had Grampap not died and the scrap yard remained, my education would have likely reached merely high school graduation, with no college. College begged to be excused as an alternative and likely to have its way. I still strongly believed that as long as it had been possible for me to work with Grampap, life would have been satisfying. I liked the thought of running the yard, but even if he'd lived, I was too young to take over its management. I'd developed the knack for knowing where to find copper and brass from stacks of dumped scrap, and that was about it. I knew nothing about keeping books, though I knew I could learn in a short time.

An endless pattern of parental internal and external abuse persisted throughout my youth. To think I could escape low-level schools existed only in a dream. Everywhere we moved, I experienced fear and intimidation from mean and oppressive boys in schools and street gangs. What did they know about their minds? Plus, Dad preferred residing in the least expensive neighborhoods, normally in a trailer on either a rented or purchased lot (never fully paid off). By Dad's choice, our nomadic existence placed us farther and farther away from people, for he hated to be near them. He believed them to be the cause of his troubles.

Nevertheless, here we were back in New Brighton, two towns from the basement we once lived in that had been the catalyst for our family madness. Both Grove City, and now New Brighton held their share of bad boys. It's not what I wanted, but what could I do except find that pipe Dad said to keep nearby?

I was born in that county and at birth weighed only five pounds. I was a small kid with skinny legs, thin arms, a small chest, and a body weight that stayed twenty or more pounds below the average kid. Even though I wouldn't discover that I had chronic, degenerative spinal stenosis for decades, it was lucky that I'd never gotten heavily into sports–the chances of a heavy impact severing my spine were huge. This, too, I felt was God being Himself, keeping me clinging to the only source of strength I knew.

The range of emotions I felt included fear, low self-confidence, hopelessness, anger, humiliation, depression, anxiety, headaches, sleep problems, body pain, and fatigue, as well as thoughts of seriously hurting my tormentors. I imagined hitting at least one, and I did. I'd met with a group of boys merely to play some basketball. This fellow kept pushing me around while on the court any time we were playing the game. I told him to stop. He refused, so I walked over to the hoop pole, picked up a pipe, and hit the kid on his back. He quit showing up for the games after that. I felt greatly relieved.

Living in New Brighton, our newest home after living only six months in Grove City, Ohio, placed us back in the county that had led Dad to flee and chase after that drunken wife of his.

A few distractions I had, one of which was my craftsmanship in a woodshop.

"You are asking for what, Brayshaw?" one New Brighton, Pennsylvania substitute teacher asked. I loved the wood shop. It was a safe space for a kid like me to be creative and keep my attention away from the anxiety and hopelessness of home.

"To be permitted to work on my rifle rack when nothing important is taking place in my appointed schedule." It was also much safer for me to be away from an unstable family, as well as mean and bigger boys. Avoiding them all was best.

"You've had this agreement with Mr. Gill, haven't you?" Mr. Gill was either taking a break from the wood shop or nearing retirement and eating up his leave time.

"Yes, sir, we worked together well. I provided for him an extra hand to clean the shop, and he permitted me time to complete my woodworking." I walked the width of the shop as I spoke, hoping the instructor would get a full idea of the size of what it was I'd been cleaning.

"Wow, I can't wait to see this project of yours. Okay, go for it, but I want this place to shine," he said, and so it did.

Once, while attending New Brighton High School, I asked to be excused to go to the restroom, and when I entered, in less than a second, a tall, muscular boy punched me very hard in the chest, knocking me to the floor. I was breathless. He stood over me, laughing with his buddies around him. I'd had no warning that the punch was coming.

From that day forward, I carried with me a large hunting knife and had it always on me in case I saw that guy again, and I truly felt I was ready to use it. The knife was sticking out of my pocket while I sat at my desk one day when a girl asked why I carried it. I explained to her that I worked in a woodshop, and I needed it for various projects.

On top of the bullying, I underwent a terrible phase lasting years, dealing with facial breakouts, another source of ridicule by the ruffians in every school I attended.

Too often, I felt vulnerable, threatened, weak, and unsafe. It would have helped if Dad had taught me to fight, but the only advice he ever gave me was to make certain I had a pipe or bat near me and to threaten the man's life.

"There's not much I can tell you. Find out on your own. You must learn to be fearless." Dad told me. "You can't let them see you're afraid of them. Hit the biggest guy one good time on a soft spot and tell him to leave you alone or you'll kill him and his entire family. That's what I do to this day. Get them before they get you. Find a pipe and use it if you must."

I remember the day Dad threw a man through a plate-glass window at a club. I didn't see it, but I overheard a discussion among Dad's friends for a week. The fellow kept pushing for it.

A friend of Dad's finally told me the whole story. "He would not leave your father alone. He tried to get money from him, always sticking his face practically in your dad's drink while he appealed to him for a few bucks. The loser pleaded, 'Come on, man, just a couple of dollars. That's all. You'll get it back, I promise. How about a twenty? I'm in the back room playing poker, losing my ass. I'm broke, and my old lady is going to be pissed. Just a twenty, man.' Then your dad said, 'Listen, buddy, I said beat it! Leave me alone. Go bother someone else!' He was about at the breaking point. So, the loser said, 'Ten, then. How about ten?' He continued for another few minutes and finally closed his fists and hit the bar table. That was it. That's when your dad grabbed the man and threw him as hard as he could.

"Your Dad wasn't looking at what was behind the guy. He hurled him through a plate-glass window. The cost for repairs, I never discovered. It wasn't tempered glass, as it would have cost him five times more to replace."

I envied my father's ability to take care of himself. He was a fighter and a good one, one who had no fear of anyone. His father, a tough railroad worker, whom Dad longed to imitate, also lived a rough life.

During my grade school years, I had a moderate talent for sports. I played with the boys in the neighborhood, especially baseball, but that petered out after Mom's incident. After that day, I lost interest in many things except for the occasional basketball game in New Brighton on an outdoor court. Athletics took a back seat, and anyway, physical education requirements had to be met. As time progressed, sports became geared toward guys who wanted to show their toughness. The naked gang showers were saturated by a constant flow of uncouth language with imitation tough guy behaviors the gym classes demanded. I despised that culture. It would get aggressively worse as the hormones raged.

That's how my thin size kept me from junior and senior high sports competitions. It made me a target of bullies throughout my public education. But then, my congenital genetic condition isn't suited for sports of any sort, except for sportsmanship endeavors like hunting and fishing during my early decades.

But it was not as if I didn't attempt anything in sports at all. I presented my weedy, emaciated body to the wrestling coach in Grove City, Ohio, in a plea to gain strength and weight by joining his team. I didn't know I would be putting my life at risk. I wouldn't discover congenital spinal stenosis until my sixties.

Dinner was hopeless. Half the time, I was starving. All that the other boys did, I followed, including running up and down the auditorium stairs to lift barbells with a weight less than that which was picked up by most of the muscular boys.

The coach would select a pair of boys from the team to get on the mat and practice their moves while the rest of the players stood around watching. Thrown onto the mat in mere seconds, my weight could not compete with the others. And yet, the coach let me stay with it, until, one day after practice, he asked me to quit.

"I can see how hard you work at it, Dave. I admire you for it." But, as he informed me, I failed to have the needed weight or size, or nutrition the other boys received from their parents.

Bullying took place in every school that I attended. "You wait until I get you off the bus," a boy from Tampa's Dowdell Junior High told me. Trying to evade him didn't work because he sat at the front of the bus. His hits forced me to ask my brother to accompany me to a school bus stop about a quarter mile from the house. To this day, I ask myself why we didn't choose to beat that kid to a pulp.

Informed by a close Tampa friend decades later, I learned that the bully who refused to stop harassing me as a young kid got his due. "He grew up to be nothing more than a strung-out junkie alcoholic who is likely dead now," Wayne told me. "All he does is sit in his house smoking dope, traipsing the neighborhood pleading for handouts." How delighted I was to hear he'd gotten his due. I wasn't a very deeply committed Christian then, yet even as I think about it today, I wish Denny and I together would have stopped the intimidations against us with a couple of maple ball bats. A lot of sleepless nights would have then ended.

In school, I'd read about a few gangs here and there in the Tampa newspaper. Nowadays, there are the Comanche Boys, Drak Boys, Dumbway, Savage Gits, Wildside, and 700 Boys. If they existed as a boy in South Tampa, I'm thankful I didn't run into them.

About my acne–there was no cure, no matter what I did. I stole tubes of ointment, squeezed the zits and blackheads, and scrubbed my face with a brush, which only aided my ugliness.

My stepmother used to have me put my head on her lap while she squeezed blackheads from all over my face, then sent me into the bathroom to use her "facial" brush. How frightfully repulsive I looked!

An older, bigger boy laughed as he said to me while we sat in Grove City's study hall, "Do you scrub your face with a wire brush?" I recognized hate when it was near me. It seemed to be just about everywhere.

When the breakouts reached my neck and shoulders, I was so embarrassed that several times I refused to go swimming. More years passed, and today a person would not suspect I had much trouble at all with my facial appearance. The truth is, the problem really does go away.

While living at Grampap's, I never gave thought to the entering of my adolescence and all that it contained. I lived in Parma for at least a year before my ugliest days. And anyway, Parma had no bullies, and because I could do anyone's homework, I used to hire my services for a few extra dollars, which made me very popular.

Grampap's death had forced me to return to my family in Tampa, and then we moved to O'Fallon, Missouri, Grove City, Ohio, and back to New Brighton, Pennsylvania. In New Brighton, I only associated with a handful of kids outside of school. With them, I played basketball in the afternoons on a cul-de-sac a few blocks from our house and in the evenings played poker in our family basement.

The unhappiness that haunted me created health issues that I struggled to hide. One most welcome hideaway, which served me well, came to me through Mr. Gill's wood shop. That's where I'd created my gorgeous mahogany rifle rack.

So, being handy, and, I suppose, thought of as nerdy, other jobs came to me on the high school campus. The electronics department asked me to roll a cart with a movie projector into classrooms whose assignment for the day included the viewing of an instructional film. Setting up a film was a cinch for me. I liked the job because it made me feel wanted and important.

In O'Fallon, Missouri, after my attempt to gain a spot on the wrestling team, I tried to get involved once more with a band. My chance to make it an impressive achievement was, once again, erased. Dad and Lou's fights in that city must have taken the lead in being the most bothersome to the police department because we were out of that city in a heartbeat. All I remember are my emerging zits and the battles that overwhelmed our household.

In New Brighton, home life contained the same alcoholic horrors. Threats by Lou of murdering us in our sleep as she wielded a knife in hand, even while Dad was present, lasted until I quit high school to enter the Navy. In that two-story home owned by two liquored-up looney tunes, the hours crept by with long nights of screaming and cursing that kept all of us kids awake.

When they were both out of the house drinking and carousing the clubs, the three of us looked through the kitchen for food to prepare, something that would leave no mess so as not to be found to have been near Lou's kitchen.

The mentality that comprised their Appalachian, alcoholic, thoughtless lives, all of which they inherited as a gift from working in and around other plastered blue-collar union workers and members of deeply entrenched booze halls, seldom created the first bit of laughter.

Many kids lived under similar circumstances. The brutality altered by degree, but all were subject to the same ingredients—the prevalence of alcohol purchased from innumerable watering holes poured into the livers of countless mothers and fathers. Twenty percent of the population were alcoholics.

Then, one day, a way of escape manifested. Denny came up with it.

"Dad, please sign these papers. They will permit me to enlist in the Navy." Denny asked as we sat around the dining room table. Hearing him, I realized I would be right behind him and hitchhiked the following day to the Rochester Post Office to retrieve enlistment papers.

Dad signed for both of us and became much relieved to have his two sons out of the way of his unhealthy attachment to that raving lunatic. He displayed either a kind of fatherly pride or an "At last they're gone" attitude while watching his boys choose the Navy above high school education.

In a little while, Denny, Diana, and I would be gone, having all enlisted. Diana chose the Air Force. That left Doug all alone as he was seven years younger than Denny and me. He lived in a motel room on Third Avenue when things got bad in New Brighton. There was little heat, so additional clothing had to be worn. Without a freezer, the groceries that had to be stored frozen were kept in a box attached to the outside window ledge.

One month later, Denny and I were sitting on a plane–my first airline experience–headed for Milwaukee, Wisconsin, from where the US Navy bused the two of us to the Great Lakes Naval Training Center.

From 1965 to 1969, my parents gave little attention to any of us kids. And so I was much relieved to be escaping that hell and looked forward to a new life ahead for me. In my possession is the county newspaper printed the day, covering our departure from Beaver County. The plane and busloads of recruits surrounding me in the aircraft were also headed for boot camp. All came from our general address, Beaver County, Pennsylvania.

Denny and I left for boot camp in 1969 while our family resided, not much longer, in New Brighton. After our boot camp graduation, we returned to Pennsylvania to find the house in New Brighton was no longer the family's residence. Dad had relocated his family to Mansell's Trailer Court along Route 51, not far from Brady's Run Park, in the late spring months of 1969. The reason for this move was the sale of the New Brighton rental.

But, before that shuffle, the house in New Brighton had to be baptized with blood and violence by the continual battles of our severely mentally deranged parents. Fights, blow-ups, screams, hunger, alcoholism, madness, blame, hatred, misery, insomnia, anxiety, fear, unhappiness, sadness, depression, and the threat of suicide grew to be the awesome symptoms of the disease that took over their lives. Not one part of it could be escaped, and no desire by Dad or Lou existed to set their intense arguments aside. The only lifestyle they understood was fueled by liquor.

Just how is Beaver County these days regarding family relations, economic challenges, and population figures?

Regarding employment, a cousin recently told me on the phone, "Things haven't been the same for some time now." He added that he'd not been employed for several years after the machine shop closed, where his bosses once raved about his performance. "You remember Tom McCay? He had a drunken wife too. He wouldn't give her up either. It cost him his house just to be rid of her. And now, all this unemployment."

"About all we have here that seems a bit promising is the Shell ethylene cracker plant being built in Monaca. It will employ only 600 people, and hire over 6,000 to build it, so once it's built and underway, it will only be a drop in a bucket for what this area needs for jobs," he added.

How well I knew the truth of that statement. It does not have to take the decline of a major industry, such as the collapse of the Jones and Laughlin Steel Company in the 1980s, to cause families to crumble when booze is so readily available.

CHAPTER 11:

Boot Camp

After surviving years of emotional abuse, I did not fathom what I was getting myself into when I followed Denny's lead. Would boot camp be rough on me? We flew to Milwaukee after a significant delay by the bus company into the Great Lakes Naval Training Center.

In boot camp, the petty officers tried to tweak my mindset, to change my way of thinking into the military frame of mind. I wondered if I'd made the right choice to enlist. It was troublesome to accept that I'd made the right choice to enlist. From the start, as we unloaded from the bus, all of us were yelled at, which created anxiety more than contentment.

I hated being pushed around. How ironic, when both my identical twin brother and I had to suffer further emotional and psychological abuse at the hands of petty officers. Hadn't we brothers had enough abuse as boys in an unsettled home and among bullying students? Here came further hell, compliments of the Navy. But stay tuned, for there is even more of this to come in every phase of my life.

One afternoon, I was shining my shoes when I thought to myself, "What is this place? What have I got myself into?" What led me to join the Navy wasn't the fear of the draft, nor was it an option given to me by police authorities to either enlist or serve time, nor did I feel particularly daring and gallant. The thoughts that led me there were of a kind of convict's escape. I was taking flight away from years of poor oversight by parents who should have had their license to raise children revoked if indeed such a bureau existed. But it didn't.

Even though I welcomed the freedom from a home saturated with despair and the loss of hope, a quantity of co-dependency existed. Horror was familiar, not the absence of it. But I welcomed getting away despite carrying into this new world some genuine depression.

So, why did I enlist? Purely to flee a bad homelife. It was difficult, too hard to act under the battling of incompetent parents, and now I was thinking I'd signed up for further abuse. Petty officers, from right off the bus, kept insulting anyone in their path.

Those in-charge wanna-bes caused me to recall the horror I'd fled—all those past thoughts and feelings compounded. I wasn't quite sure how to react. It would have been nice to have been given a booklet on How To Survive Naval Training with something more than how to wash, fold and put away one's clothes and gear. How was I to know what I was permitted to say? I learned to react less and to pay attention to what was said to me. Sarcasm and mockery were tempters, but I pushed them aside.

And so, my initial introduction to the Navy grew to be nothing more than me contemplating my past while following the sailor ahead of me, in one line after another, each step aiding my escape from hell. I looked forward to a new life, something different that took my attention from the anxieties that accompanied the decreasing presence of dysfunction.

Not much farther than getting my vaccinations, booster shots, penicillin shots, and several others I don't recall, things would change, but not before they cut my hair nearly bald. I got up a lot earlier than I was accustomed, which took some getting used to. The drill instructors never ceased their humiliating put-downs and degrading insults.

Then came that happy surprise. Those in charge discovered I could type forty-five words per minute, which made me a candidate to work as the MIC Petty Officer clerk. They called the division MIC by its nickname, "Mickey Mouse." In today's Navy boot camp, the name for MIC is "Manager's Internal Control," sort of like a school for slow-to-catch-on types. As the instructor's clerk, I was relieved of all the usual workouts and drills. The recruits placed in MIC found what most of us would consider ordinary to be a big challenge for them, such as the correct way to make a rack (bunk bed), fold clothes, do laundry, smoke (in the days when designated smoking lamps existed indoors), ironing, bathing, report on time to training, and shining shoes.

Leading each unit was a male Petty Officer (PO) whose duties were to handle the welfare, behavior, and military education of the recruits assigned to him. Throughout the period of initial training, these non-commissioned officers looked for a certain type of character in a recruit. For instance, when a young man or woman was timid, or wasn't sure of himself, they reacted against him, an entirely opposite reaction than I would have chosen. The kid needed care, not condemnation. The lesson for timidity was for a recruit to always scream out answers, all answers, even if the petty officer being addressed stood near.

I recall the day I taught a timid recruit that his best response to all petty officers was to loudly blast the reply no matter the distance from him. For instance, when being asked his name, I told the recruit to scream, "Chief Petty Officer, the recent enlistee's name is David Drake." Above all, I strongly insisted recruits never say "Sir" to a petty officer who was noncommissioned.

My duties as a clerk included overseeing the paperwork associated with the petty officer's position. Once assigned to MIC, I was obliged to send to every parent their son's change in plans. They were being relocated to MIC, which would delay their graduation day by three months.

That was just one of my assignments besides shuffling papers to keep this man's reputation intact. I also had to guide the recruits to and from certain out-of-barracks activities, to do roll calls, to attend chow, and to remind them of all things related to their daily schedules.

The organization of materials challenged me. I never imagined so much written communication existed. Overseers could have introduced me to the forms I was to work with through a short educational program prior to sending me into MIC, but instead, they threw me into an office with an unsympathetic and merciless wanna-be who thought I understood everything about my job without the first bit of instruction. Still, I kept the PO ahead of the game, even while he declined to offer a hint of forgiveness and compassion. To his thinking, I suppose, my age, seventeen, mattered. I didn't have what it would take, even though writing had, for decades, been a strong suit of mine. In his mind, I entered the military as a backwoods redneck typist, not as an above-average-intelligence student.

To inform parents of their son's postponement, I mistakenly addressed a letter to the wrong home address, informing the parents that a recruit with a different name than their son fell upon misfortune. The father of the recruit started contact with the drill instructor to clear things up. Did his son get transferred into MIC or not? Late at night, the unit's petty officer returned to his office, awakened me, and told me to search for the names of MIC recruits.

The name I typed in that letter had me puzzled. And yet, the address I applied to that report was on our hometown list. I do not know how that man's name, with the wrong home address, got on anything I kept at my desk. But it did, causing all hell to break loose. I later discovered the error got to me by mistake, created by those who assigned my workload. The fault lay with the staff above me, not me. Still, I was to be punished.

"Brayshaw! What in the hell have you gotten me into?"

"I'm not sure, Petty Officer," I spoke as I looked down to the tiled floor, then the mass of papers I felt I'd be rummaging through within the next few minutes.

"I was planning to suggest assigning you to yeoman's school, but today you are in a world of shit! Write up an apology and send it to the parents you lied to. This is for fucking up. You're lucky you only have a short time remaining in this office, or I would have you removed. Are you listening to me, recruit? For your graduation duty assignment, you will be sent aboard a destroyer as a deck ape. There will be no yeoman school for you. You will swab decks until you're discharged. Do you understand?"

"Yes, I do, Petty Officer." Would there be no real successes for me in this life? I wondered. At this point, I thought the definite answer was "No."

From that time on, I did not exist to that man. Only the most necessary details did he permit me to perform. I escorted the men to chow and reminded them of their normal daily duties. For the rest of the term, I got the silent treatment.

True to his word, my appointment to a duty station turned out to be aboard a destroyer out of Mayport, Florida. Little did he know, the same assignment as a boatswain's mate seaman also went to my twin brother and stepbrother. Tony enlisted at least a year before us, so he was soon to arrive at homeport from a Westpac cruise. He'd been to Vietnam, I thought, and would have plenty to talk about. To have both alongside me, I would thrive, I told myself.

In the years that followed my graduation, Navy officials extended boot camp training to ten weeks, adding an extra two weeks to overall training. I understand the Navy added more mentorship, life skills, and personal and professional development to its boot camp after realizing those skills were underdeveloped within most crews.

I'm glad I wasn't around to be forced to endure an additional two weeks working for that childish petty officer. I understand the Army no longer allows drill sergeants to cuss, rant, abuse, or threaten recruits. They cannot slap, hit, kick, punch, or call recruits names any longer. Is it the same for the Navy? I wonder.

A good site to learn how today's boot camp operates is to watch Austen Alexander's YouTube videos. He grew up in Florence, Alabama, dropped out of college to join the Navy in 2013, and spent seven years as Naval Security (MA) working in Harbor Patrol. I learned a good bit from him, especially regarding titles and physical training. How Navy boot camp operates today is far from my indoctrination.

In one situation, Seaman Recruit Alexander preferred wearing contacts over eyeglasses and was told to set his contacts aside and never again bring them out or wear them. They provided him Navy Government Issue eyeglasses, and they would have to suit him. While being led to a final day ceremony, this recruit thought he looked better with contacts, which he retrieved and inserted. While being taken to the facility to meet up with other divisions, an RDC asked if he'd removed his glasses and inserted contacts.

"Yes, Recruit Division Commander."

"Everyone, listen up. Seaman Recruit Alexander here has distracted his company from their intended mission. He disobeyed a direct order. All of you will get down, NOW! Give me fifty pushups."

The company ended up doing three sets of fifty before their punishment was complete. The company missed the event.

How ironic that in today's Navy, commanding officers are using courts-martial as a corrective device more frequently than in pre-war days. They do not realize that many courts being given are actually a reflection of the officers' command ability, not the shipmates' extreme inability.

"We still have pretty decent training standards, but we don't get punished like the others," said one E-4. In the same breath, however, he said that "Today's RDCs play mind games to mess up the recruit. For instance, one of our RDCs made us put backpacks on and off our racks about 100 times when somebody forgot theirs.

"The cure is to work as a team," said Alexander. "Things will go much easier. Help the guy who is less cognizant of the commands. Don't be an individual. Do everything you can to succeed in a unit. It is best to stay motivated and know that you have it in yourself to get through the training."

CHAPTER 12:

Military Tour Overseas

At every port where the Noa moored or docked, a common itinerary existed in the minds of the crew. They had a good idea of where they were destined once the ship got tied up and liberty was called. Exceptions existed.

We'd just docked in Karachi, Pakistan.

"Hey, where's my razor I loaned you?" asked Doug Losey. He was about to hop in the shower and noticed I'd dropped items into my douchebag while standing at the head sink. "I saw it a couple of days ago. I must have it below," I said.

A few inches shorter than me, with dark hair, a mustache, and exceptionally good-natured, Doug's Milwaukee caring upbringing fit well his duties as the paint locker manager. Proof that he was rooted in a well-loved environment showed in his character and gentle devotion to serving others. He kept his station in good shape and earned a third-class boatswain's mate (BM) promotion after a couple of years. On off-duty hours, we enjoyed automobile restoration in the on-base garage set up for sailors' personal use. The heaps we worked on, we bought for next to nothing.

Despite a stark contrast to our previous home lives, our friendship lasted a lifetime. Desolately, I cried for days immediately after hearing he died of a brain aneurysm three years ago. I still miss him, and no wonder. He was to me as close as a brother. During the last visit that Denny and I had with him, I discovered some startling news. Down from Milwaukee, he rented a house for an entire week and brought along his entire family. That's when I learned the particulars of his disease.

Our talks led to his revelation that both of his brothers had passed from the same condition. From a stable family life, he brought into the Navy a rare stability I envied, which obviously helped to promote his rank. While he moved up the ladder, I kept falling off it, adopting attitudes that reflected the hard, troubled life I endured as a boy. For me, I was able to easily see the flaws in that day's naval system, but for Doug, life was good and fair. He saw everything, as I once heard sung, "through rose-colored glasses."

"I owe you a new one. Gillette? Just give me a day. I'll find it. I'll tell you what. You quit puffing on those damn Winstons, and I'll buy you a store full of blades." Like his brothers, he too smoked plenty, although his death was not related to cigarettes, which is another one of life's ironies. Each brother, born with the same congenital condition, smoked as much as the other two, but it was a hidden condition that promoted their deaths.

"Where are you going tonight? I hope it's not to get drunk, is it?" Doug asked. He said that, knowing well that liquor seldom touched my lips. Oh, we'd put down a six-pack on occasion while working on our cars, but that was about it.

Doug knew well the distance I kept from alcohol, even though, a few times, we looked in on the guys who preferred to spend all their time in the bars and cat houses. During those stopovers with the rest of the crew, we pretended to support their overindulgences. Twice drunk was enough for me.

Whether to drink or wander about the town, I still had a lot of scrubbing to do on my face and arms before I could leave after I ground down the non-slip deck, covering the length of half the central passageway leading to the barbershop.

A moderate breeze coming in through the open hatches caused the black grit to stick to my sweaty body like a roll of flypaper. Without them open, the hatches would seal in the grinder's noise, which helped to create, for some sailors, serious hearing problems. Today, I wear hearing aids and listen day and night to the ringing in my ears. The tinnitus is a constant reminder of my naval duties.

"A walk, I need, Doug," I said, "to release my muscles from all that grinding, bending, and twisting the lieutenant had me doing. The cramped space caused my legs to ache."

"Then what? Where are you going, to some dumpy bar?" he asked. The steamy mirror, he wiped to see better.

"I'm considering grabbing a buggy with Tony and checking out some jewelry shops. It's his idea." And it certainly was, for I was in the dark regarding Tony's true intent. I thought it would be a nice gesture to purchase a gift for my mother and sister, something not expensive, and have the gems made into necklaces. But every time Tony was able to get the jeweler to turn his head or to walk to the back in search of an item, he grabbed handfuls of topaz, sapphires, and opals.

I wanted none of that and excused myself by pretending I spotted fellow shipmates who seemed lost wandering outdoors.

For most of the crew, shore leave, or liberty meant one thing. To get drunk and laid. In fact, a brothel was the destination for most shipmates who walked ashore. Sailors who had never been to a foreign port normally followed the old salts. It was part of most shipmates' indoctrination.

From what I saw, I believed there were fewer beer halls established for the sake of dropping in to have a beer than there were clubs where women plied their trades in order to earn a livelihood.

In many ports, especially in Bombay, India, pimps partitioned long carts pulled by oxen into small spaces just large enough for women to lie in as they pulled the cart on the road and the driver declared his wares.

Once sailors stumbled upon such sites, the buggy owner attempted to rent his stock of women. Many sailors refused to oblige because they judged how the women were treated. It resembled imprisonment, not a legitimate business.

In most foreign cities, women in taverns grew to be a major part of the evening, especially among seamen. They provided a release for the crew, though too many of those women were victims of forced prostitution. They lay inside small cubicles for one of two reasons: their husbands wanted them earning a living or because of their husbands' indebtedness. Part of the load contained prey for the prostitution trade.

"Did you hear what some men witnessed tonight?" I asked Dave Richards. We had joined up as Black and White photography hobbyists and often worked well into the evening hours, rolling negatives in the pitch darkness of the foc'sle below.

"No, what happened?" he asked. Dave's inquisitiveness often led him onto an important story, worthy of publication, if we only had pictures. But the topic would not sit well with the wives of sailors who read military periodicals.

"Mac spotted a wagon load of boxed-in slave prostitutes. You wanna go catch a story here?" One of my thoughts for life following my enlistment was to learn to write for newspapers. Sadly, that profession would, in another decade, be wiped out once computers took over. But how did I know? I kept my dream alive by writing short articles that earned me next to nothing from various publications.

Had I possessed the same leaning toward journalism as I did in later years, photos of those women and the attention they aroused might have earned me a couple of dollars with the right magazine editor.

John overheard me talking to Dave about his sightings in Bombay. "Yeah, man, he's right. I saw young women in cages. Can you believe it–cages? Men, young and old, watched as the women waved and lifted their skirts. The women were merchandise, picked out like a half a pound of ham."

I'd spent enough time talking about boxes with cages and chose to flee the ship before liberty ended. And anyway, I couldn't get over how double-minded Islamic austerity was. It was a sham because sex was for sale in every bar. While the authorities jailed couples who kissed in Bahrain, the State turned a blind eye to 30,000 imported prostitutes.

I was slowly getting off the ship and sat with a handful of fellow sailors on the fantail as we talked about home. Our talk proved the irony of a shipmate's life, how much he missed the water when the ship wasn't cruising. At the same time, he missed being home, to be on shore doing whatever hobby kept him devotedly busy. Some built boats while others fished to their hearts' content. In addition to the ocean waters, numerous leisure interests existed in the hearts of Navy seamen.

The next day, while working the flight deck, I looked out at the harbor and did a double take. Men were holding hands with other men.

"Look, look over there, fellows. Do you see those men holding hands?" I asked. Three sailors, one of whom was my brother, were below the fantail when they heard me and climbed the ladder topside to look.

"I spotted the same thing a couple of days ago," Denny said. "The chaplain said it is the only way affection can be shown in Islamic countries while in public. Men aren't allowed to touch a woman around others. A public show of affection toward a woman is an offense worthy of arrest."

Such an odd custom, I thought, when prostitution was so easily accessible. What man wouldn't want to hold the hand of the one he loved? I said, "Such a custom is primitive. You can't make a law against what is so natural."

"We're not in Mayport, that's for sure," another shipmate, Ben, said. He was one of the few guys who bore a tattoo. That custom, which is, today, so very common, wasn't supported, but there was a good reason for it. A seaman could be placed on report for destroying public property if he was found bearing a tattoo on his body.

Doug joined us on the fantail. "Hey, Doug," I said. "I hear your brother will be joining us soon. He wants this life too. Wow, now that makes two sets of brothers sharing a duty station."

"Yea, he completed boot camp and asked to be stationed here with me on the Noa." I thought this meant even more help working on our cars and that Roger must know as much as Doug.

How different the Navy was changing under Admiral Zumwalt. The rules were much more relaxing under his watch to the approval of most men. Brothers onboard with other brothers put most sailors in mind of the five Sullivan brothers, World War II sailor brothers of Irish American descent who served together on the light cruiser USS Juneau.

They were all killed in action in and after it sank around November 13, 1942. Most American families thought their deaths would put an end to relatives serving aboard the same vessel. It did for a while, but now the custom was back.

To my shipmates, I confessed that there were, at one time, three brothers who shared duty stations on the Noa, but the stepbrother deserted. "Our stepbrother, Tony, refused to stay once back from Nam," I said.

I told them that something happened that caused him to flee in a flash—a wife. "Being married to a particularly beautiful woman made it hard for him. He couldn't trust her to stay away from other men. I doubt it will work for them in the long run. He's too jealous." Not long after he jumped ship, Darlene shut her doors to him and let the divorce papers go through channels.

The policy to allow for kin gained favor with the sailors who had brothers eligible to enlist. Others didn't mind too much. The Navy no longer objected to family members serving on the same ship, but there was a catch. Either one of them could be transferred to a different vessel or a shore station, which the brothers seldom gave a thought to. It was the Navy's way of gaining men that carried conditions.

The atmosphere of these Middle Eastern cities I did not know, either by books I'd read or the viewing of movies I watched as a boy. Some films used Middle Eastern countries as backdrops for films. I recall Peter Sellers' role as a comedic, bumbling Pakistani, but that was the full extent of my knowledge of Middle Eastern culture and dialect.

As I walked the streets of Pakistan, the scent of the restaurants blew me away. The aroma of Pakistani meat dishes, normally killed at the stand and cooked, wafted down the avenues, overtaking all other vendors, even India's veggie dishes. Pakistanis are massive meat eaters. They consume three times more meat than all of India. At the same time, Indian chefs knew how to cook vegetables like no other eateries in the world. Therefore, I purchased vegetable dishes at Pakistani restaurants and meat from Indian vendors.

While chewing, I noticed a large group of Pakistanis gathering on the other side of the street. Was a party going on? "What's up over there?" I asked one of the resting buggy owners.

I was fortunate to discover he knew English, this short, rather talkative man to whom the notion of peace seemed not to exist. I learned he'd been in a heated exchange that turned out to be nothing more than a simple glass of water for a rider.

The conversation between the business owner and the driver was passionate. This is how I learned later that Pakistani culture is very expressive. Whatever they love, they do with plenty of zest and excitement, even normal conversation.

"What's going on?" I asked. The voices across the street grew louder.

"The people there?" He seemed to act bothered.

"Yea, what's going on?"

A wedding, he told me, was underway. Relatives and friends were just arriving, decked out from head to toe.

I asked him about the music that I heard being played, which opened a brief discussion on preferences. Being much into country music since my earliest days, he nodded when I mentioned a tune he recognized.

"Johnny Cash," he said. "I hear that train comin', coming' round the tracks." I laughed calmly to acknowledge his span of familiarity.

I clapped at his imitation and failed to compete, for I knew nothing of his country's music. What I heard coming from that gathering across the street wasn't country at all, but odd-sounding, high-toned music that set the pace for the ceremony.

He listed a few Indian and Pakistani genres: Balti, Punjabi, Potohari, Sindhi, and the instruments used. I knew of only three instruments he mentioned, all three of them used in country music. The other instruments he brought up were the rubab, dholak, and tabla.

Dave and I listened for some time to the music, then left to inspect the other shops.

Another comparison, easy to notice, was Pakistani cleanliness. Their food preparation areas shined when compared to that of their vegan counterparts.

City designs were similar. The difference that stood out most, I found, was that people on the street in Pakistan were more helpful, although some travel guides will admit today is different.

I've been told that their culture teaches Pakistanis to be wary of foreigners. My experience did not prove that in the 70s. But then, in those several days, I spent more time on the streets with Pakistanis than I did with Indians. One Pakistani buggy driver took Tony, a fellow sailor, and me, through the city to inspect jewelry shops, which he heard were affordable. For the cab fare, all the driver wanted was a copy of Playboy, one of which I found among the division's scattered "reading" material.

Maybe it is true. Maybe Indians today are even warmer than in times past.

Several other obvious differences between the two cultures, I easily noticed. British English usage was more prevalent in India. Pakistan had less poverty, and the streets were cleaner. There were hardly any stray animals in Pakistan. About driving a car, I observed that Pakistanis drove safer, but the fines were strict. Not entirely surprising to me is that Pakistan had no liquor stores. India had more women in the streets than Pakistan. And women in India were more approachable.

While in these countries in the 70s, Indians were permitted to piss along the streets in public but were not allowed to kiss. Such laws, I asserted, were ludicrous.

At one of the dancing stage show brothels, one woman announced to all the sailors that any of the women whores would do anything the customer wanted for $135 for an entire evening. That declaration had taken place in a brothel, not on the sidewalks in town. The whores had something to offer to the right patron, but I wanted more to understand the culture of the people as opposed to fulfilling a longtime naval tradition.

Not just sailors consented to join in the alcoholic-filled evenings and fornication, for even the most unexpected civilians took part. One of these adulterers hid his iniquity from others for years. It wasn't until he died that the truth came out. He was a well-respected U.S. Christian leader who paid the apartment rent of a prostitute for his sole pleasure.

This man, whom I once looked forward to hearing, gave talks behind podiums on auditorium stages throughout the world. His messages had a strong leaning toward logic more than they did the actual preaching of the gospel. The discipline is known as apologetics, an academic approach to the proof of God's existence.

He paid one such woman in Taiwan in the tens of thousands, affording her a home and a good life while she awaited his return. His ministry, following his exposure, changed leadership and the ministry's emphasis and is now helping abused women.

His family requested, upon realizing the full truth of their founder's escapades, all the books he'd written that remained on the library shelves of Christians around the world to be tossed into the trash or burned.

The islands we visited in the middle of the Indian Ocean were startling, especially the Seychelle Islands. The beauty was breathtaking. Also, there was Port Louis, Mauritius. One sailor admitted, "The first time there, I got drunk at a bar called the Blue Moon. On the second night, the community invited us to a dance at the Embassy. We jumped on it because we thought there would be girls. It turned out, they were only teenagers, and it was more like a church social. We left that group as soon as we realized there would be no partying." How sad for those people, after going to such lengths to welcome Americans to their island.

Dangerous incidents occurred as well. In Dakar, Senegal, sailors could have been killed if a police officer had not come by. It was only a day or two after Charles de Gaulle passed away.

Said one petty officer, "The day de Gaulle died, they moored us at a French port. It was another country in mourning, just as we had experienced with Robert Kennedy's and Martin Luther King's assassinations.

"The crew of 1st Division went out to some bar, got drunk, and when it was time to leave, we got into the wrong cab, not the first in line. Bad words were uttered and then somebody said something about De Gaulle, and a fight broke out. Cops came, and the embassy got involved in something one of the big shots labeled an international incident. We went straight to Captain's Mast and everyone involved was put on two weeks extra duty."

A near-deadly incident took place, according to Gene Levine, a sailor from the USS Noa (DD-841). "A bunch of us were sitting at a bar in Victoria, Seychelles. A local opened up the side door floors above us and heaved a very large rock that hit a shipmate, Bruce, on the top of his head. It happened so fast, and everybody ran outside to see if the perpetrator would show himself, but he was long gone.

"You talk about some pissed-off sailors. I honestly think if they would have caught the guy responsible, they would have beaten him to death. Bruce was bleeding profusely from his head, and if you saw the size of that rock, it's a miracle it didn't kill him or knock him out."

In Thailand, an even more highly esteemed sex destination existed known as "Sin City." In fact, that nightlife hub was famous for its sex industry, which grew day by day. And yet, that location, known as Pattaya, remained a tourist favorite, one of the most sought-after destinations for servicemen.

Today, times have changed. In 2006, the Department of Defense made it a crime for a service member to hire a prostitute anywhere in the world; the penalties today include up to a year in prison, forfeiture of pay, and a dishonorable discharge.

While back on the ship, I encountered Dave, my hobby buddy. "Maybe we can do some timed photography tonight; Dave, would you like that?" I asked.

"Nah, I spent enough time reeling onto spools negatives from the shots we took the night before. I'm headed for my rack."

I understood him well. Sleep was important. Not getting enough could put a lookout in need of a few cups of strong caffeine before he headed for his scheduled watch, and God forbid a man was caught sleeping on watch, especially in locations hidden from most of the crew, such as aft lookout.

Speaking to Doug, prior to his passing several years ago, I learned he grew to be a most trusted employee in his civilian workplace. Frequently he was called out to the hardest repair jobs ever to cross the boss' desk. Overtime kept him away from his charming, beautiful wife, Annie, who I eventually met many years later.

CHAPTER 13:

After our leaving

Dad left New Brighton after his rental home was sold. He relocated to Mansell's Trailer Court down the backside of Beaver Falls, Pennsylvania, working off and on as the union provided work.

Denny and I left Pennsylvania for the Navy, while, months later, Diana enlisted in the Air Force. Without any warning, Lou fled to Florida with an unknown man she met in a bar and haunted Dad with calls that boasted of her exit to make him jealous. The next step came easy for Dad. He chased after her taking along with him his ten-years old son, Doug, who he dropped off at numerous homes of step relatives and friends, as he pursued the most worthless alcoholic on the face of the earth. To this day, Doug greatly dislikes being reminded of how he was treated like a pet that needed to be boarded every time Dad's purposes would not fit him.

Lou was completely attached to the Hitching Post in South Tampa, where she met this man who traveled to Pennsylvania to convince her to run off with him. Dad spotted them and confronted Lou's drinking partner/lover with a promise to break his legs. That put an end to her games. Absent any justifiable reason, Dad took her back, but it would not last long. A couple more towns later, they would finally end their terror-filled relationship.

Dad rented a trailer to the west of his former location on El Camino. The lot contained a clean, well-kept, abandoned trailer, but it was sitting next to an old block house that appeared unsafe. Blocks stuck out of the walls and the roof was half caved in.

It was just fine. Dad took it. Our naval enlistment was about to expire when Denny and I chose to drive southwest to visit Dad in Tampa.

Soon, Lou's brother, Frank, his wife, Doris, and daughter, Sabrina, came to live with Dad. A few of the kids slept outside or in Frank's camper truck. Frank's visit introduced me to what I learned to term functional alcoholism. In later years, I played music in beer joints, clubs, and tiki bars for over two decades along the Florida Gulf Coast. I learned no one could out-drink Frank at any time of the day. He brought his family to Florida to search for work, and he found it, as did Denny and me. Four of us rode to the job site together to work on the Gandy Bridge. I twisted rods used to strengthen the concrete. Every morning and every day after work, Frank would buy a fifth of Old Crow from a liquor store, from the same store on our route to and from work.

Frank and Doris didn't get along well either and began to speak profanities to one another, so Doris decided to return to Missouri and live in Grampap's house. The saddest part of their stay with us was the murder of their daughter, Sabrina, who remained in Missouri while her parents were visiting Florida. While taking a walk, she was kidnapped and murdered by two or three men after they dragged her into a barn and raped her. It took years for the police to find the three perpetrators, but they finally did, and each one was sentenced to life in prison.

I returned to my apartment in Neptune Beach, Florida, struggling on a pauper's livelihood to complete a college degree. Dad's next move was to Homosassa Springs, then Crystal River, a most beautiful setting adjacent to a sparkling lagoon.

Denny and I visited him there once while on leave and spent most of our time snorkeling in the caves below the crystal-clear lagoon water. It was an amazing site, full of various colors of fish and a radiating peace. It was one of God's special places.

The best part of that location was, of course, the snorkeling and sleeping outside under the stars. I had for years thought that no place on land displayed the speckles in the sky as equally bright as they did when I was cruising the Indian Ocean (USS Noa (DD-841). Crystal River was a close second. I recall well looking up at the blanket of stars that stretched across the vastness of the sky. The sight stood out, far beyond mere beauty.

By then, the house fighting grew dangerous. One afternoon, while living in that mobile in Crystal River, Florida, Dad and Doug were working in the back room when Lou began to shoot at them through the door.

"Lay on the floor," Dad said, "and place your feet against the bottom. Put all your pressure into it!" Lou's shots reached the higher part of the door. Had she lowered her aim, she would have murdered both my brother and father. "Press hard, Doug, don't let her in. There's no telling how many bullets she has!"

After this event, Dad refused to file a police report against Lou. The atmosphere returned, once again, to a quieter existence. The outbreaks of madness could be heard for blocks, which caught the notice of the police. An air of hostility continued to exist between those two lunatics. Once again, Lou retrieved her gun.

While Dad was visiting a friend on the other side of the lagoon, Denny strove out of the trailer door and walked along the water's edge toward the trailer where Dad was sitting when Lou shot at him, emptying the entire six shots in his direction. Did drunkenness, a strong mental imbalance, or another form of insanity lead her to do that?

"What did I just hear?" I asked Denny as I was lying on an outside cot. I urgently rushed inside to inspect the interior and spotted Lou with the pistol in her hand.

"Put that away, now!" I shouted.

She laid it at the bottom of a vanity drawer and acted as if her true intention did not exist. Shooting at someone, anyone, I suppose, was one of her great pleasures.

Dad ran back to his place, threw open the door, and asked about the noise. "Were you shooting, Lou? Were you trying to kill one of us? Where is that gun? I want it now, in my hands." Lou pulled back the vanity door, and there it lay. Dad grabbed and unloaded it and threw it into the middle of the lagoon. The police arrived at the insistence of the neighbors.

Discovering from the union that they needed Dad's high level of welding skills; he was hired to help build the Crystal River Power Plant. A lovely spot near the springs contained a fully furnished mobile home for rent at a reasonable price, which is where they moved. Dad bought a boat and when Denny and I went to visit, we took it out to the deep blue underwater cavern to dive into a tropical fish filled wonder.

Finally, having no more patience with one another, Lou and Dad divorced. And still, that drunken alcoholic refused to leave him alone. Dad remained at his home and refused to respond to Lou's outrageous behaviors as he continued to work on the power plant.

The power plant position was close to completion when, luckily, while speaking to a Pennsylvania buddy on the phone, Dad was told of a four-and-a-half acre piece of property for sale in the most ideal location, in Negley, Ohio, where he would remain with a third wife after he, at last, was free of Lou.

The news of their breakup didn't reach me for a good many months, or even years, after it took place. His third wife, Syd, stayed by Dad's side displaying a genuine love blended with mill-town sarcasm. They were together for a long stretch until Dad died at age 77 of lung cancer. Syd sold the property to a small business land developer and moved into a retirement home, which she detested. In conversations with Syd, she said not one of her relatives paid any attention to her by calling or sending letters. She suffered during her stay in that residence, living in limited space with others who were taking the last few steps of their lives.

For readers interested in knowing just how Lou's life evolved after having split with Dad, she, along with her two sons, Tony and Tom Eiceman, moved to Bradenton Beach, Florida to an apartment complex. They remained there for a few years, with Lou and Tony continuing in a deeply alcoholic state. A five-gallon container of Jim Beam that contained a pump was kept in Tony's bedroom from which he filled his pocket flasks for his daily indulgences. They later relocated to Chiefland, Florida, and it is there that the worst of their later years took place.

My brother, Denny, and his wife, Sherelle, visited our former family trio in the summer of 2000. As they were sitting in the living room of a double-wide trailer in Chiefland, with the company of his former stepbrother in his presence, Tony was extremely depressed after the recent passing of his brother, Tom, due to diabetes. Tony and his girlfriend knew Tom was about to die, so she snuck into the hospital all the wrong foods that Tom had kept from eating for years as he knew he was fading. Foods like fried chicken and chocolate bars were his favorite.

Tony's depression led him to first offer Denny one of his favorite 45 caliber handguns as a gift, and as they sat talking, Tony leaned his head to the corner of the couch. Rolling to the front of the sofa with his arm, he reached under the cushions to retrieve his .22 caliber handgun with which he shot himself just below the heart. An ambulance was called by Sherelle. The Emergency Management Technicians took him to the Bradenton hospital, where he stayed for months. As soon as he got into the ambulance, Denny and Sherelle departed.

For several years to follow, Tony's condition continued to decline as he remained in his home. He ate a lot; in fact, he far over-indulged, which caused a weight gain of over 340 lbs.

Lou died of cirrhosis of the liver in Gainesville at the age of 71 after a brief illness, which left Tony residing alone. It's been reported to me by one of my former stepcousins that Tony refused to go out of his place of residence except for emergencies. Groceries were delivered to him. After some time, his weight gain and alcoholism led to his demise. Born on November 9, 1950, he died at age 53 on April 4, 2004.

Dad's new location placed him away from the former police authorities whose oversight regarding everything from traffic violations to disturbances was unconscionably excessive. None of us, once we grew old enough to drive and were kept informed of the facts, liked Pennsylvania's governmental policies. The state is a commonwealth and has the 13th highest gasoline tax in the nation, at 32.3 cents per gallon. That is more than double the New Jersey gas tax. It also leads the nation in the number of structurally deficient bridges, and the roads are full of potholes everywhere one drives. So, neither Dad nor his kids ever liked Pennsylvania. Negley, Ohio, located just beyond the Pennsylvania/Ohio border, was very rural property and remains agrestic to this day. It immensely suited Dad and his untamable ways.

While on military leave, I stayed with Dad in his hideaway home. As I saw it, the location was not, in any way, a place I could call home. The trailer reeked of the most unpleasant smell of sulfur water from one end of his residence to the other. To take a shower was a torturous ordeal.

For water to drink, he and his wife filled used plastic milk containers with clean mountain spring water from a source that ran through a pipe inserted into the hillside not far from their land. Up to twenty containers would fill a trunk bed or car hatchback for the duration of each haul. I helped fill those plastic water bottles a few times while on visit.

Dad continued to drive across the border, where he would sit and bull-shit with fellow friends at the Monaca American Legion. All of them were either working or had worked in one of the many industrial plants and major construction sites within southwestern Pennsylvania.

Beaver County has evolved over the past decades. At one time, it was a very intense blue-collar industrial magnet for those in search of employment in factories, plants, mills, foundries, and various industries; today, it no longer has jobs. Male high school students from Beaver and adjacent Pennsylvania counties used to be able to gain employment as apprentices of steel, glass, propane, pipes, or chemicals, so school dropouts grew to be common. Employees failed to prepare for anything other than a plant.

CHAPTER 14:

Doug's life

I lost a lot of history that had taken place in my young brother Doug's life after Denny, Diana, and I enlisted in the Navy. We had no choice but to leave him behind, which caused him to feel abandoned and unwanted. All I could see, my own salvation from that household of terror, clung to my mind. I needed to press into a new life and that's what the Navy gave me. It put my mind in another realm, although I kept in mind what I'd run from, and wondered if any of their evil antics would cease.

After Denny and I went off to defend our country, I worried about Doug's feelings of abandonment. He was left alone to endure the battles within a war that seemed never to end. Discovering Lou's destination was simple. She missed the Hitching Post, so that became Dad's destination. Dad carted along Doug, but when they reached Tampa, he dropped him off at a friend's house.

"I can't remember them," Doug said. "It was some middle-aged man and his wife. I must have been there for ten days or more." That's when Dad decided he needed more time to make his decision about Lou. So, he drove Doug up to Jacksonville Beach, dropped him off at Denny's house, and fled the scene.

For work, Doug became a dishwasher for the Atlantic Beach Sea Turtle restaurant and hotel. One of the men at work said his dog had given birth to puppies, which seemed the ideal pet for Doug. He always loved dogs. The name he gave to the male golden retriever was Caesar. I recall him well. Such a dog everyone should have an experience living with. Caesar was gentle, lovingly protective, and added joy to Doug's life.

"I bought a 1965 Rambler that ate up a quart of oil a week and smoked like crazy. It got me around, so I didn't complain." It truly was in rough shape, but Doug was very handy and kept it on the road.

The second job he had was again dishwashing for a Ponderosa Steakhouse.

He kept that Rambler for at least a couple of years and even drove it north to Ohio, with Caesar, when Dad finally came to his senses and pushed Lou out of his life.

On his drive to Negley, Doug stopped off at Mt. Vernon, being tired and worn, at a restaurant where he met a dairy farmer's daughter. She convinced him to work for her Dad bailing hay and milking cows, and even married the girl.

"She had a young boy from another relationship who needed discipline very badly," he said. He tried being that for the kid, but his wife didn't allow it. In fact, the whole house was set against him acting as a mature twenty-year-old, so he demanded a divorce.

He then drove to Negley, reunited with Dad and his new wife, Syd, and from there married again.

"All relationships have rough patches," he said recently. "I make the best of it, realizing when it's time to call it quits, that's it. It's all over."

CHAPTER 15:

Diana's Journey

As I walked into boot camp at the Great Lakes Naval Training Center, my mind was filled with thoughts that I'd left behind a sister and brother who were to endure that hell alone, without my twin brother or me around to help soften the constant mayhem.

A year lapsed, at which time Diana chose to enlist in the Air Force, ridding her of the presence of the family madness. That choice she didn't make alone. The insistence on getting out of the house was entirely by Lou's command. On the very day Diana graduated high school, Lou approached Diana to tell her she had to leave the trailer and get out on her own, without a car and without anyone to put her up.

"I walked to Uncle Roy's house," Diana told me. "He lived where we were parked, in Mansell's Trailer Court. His wife, Kathryn, was ironing when I walked in to tell her what Lou demanded of me. Lou spoke all she did to me even as Dad looked on without comment. Evidently, he was in favor of me leaving as well." Kathryn suggested Diana enlist in the Air Force and offered to drive her to the recruiting office in Rochester that minute.

"When I went in to take the test, I passed but was told by the recruiter that I couldn't go in until November, and it was only June," Diana added, with a tone of desperation she felt regarding the delay.

"I had to stay in that trailer for another several months and avoided Lou during that time as much as possible," she remarked with memories of the discomfort streaming from her voice.

Those months passed, and barely one word was exchanged between those two.

Diana, at that time, had a boyfriend, Sean, to whom she felt obligated to inform him regarding her plans. She did not talk to him right away for fear of him turning away from her. "He gave me his ring, and I never told him I was going into the military."

"What did you do with the ring?" I asked, thinking she must have liked it a great deal since she owned no jewelry of her own.

"I sent it back to him while I was in basic training," she said.

She also failed to tell her best friend, Carlene, about her plans. Had she told her, Carlene's family would have put her up, potentially for the remainder of the years necessary for her to develop plans.

Her initial response upon entering the service was equal to mine. "I liked the Air Force immediately," Diana admitted, "because we got three meals a day, and they made me feel safe and secure, something I never felt at home. In fact, I should have stayed in." She was performing exceptionally at her station and was about to be reassigned to an Alaskan post. Regrettably, she chose to marry a man who demanded that she refuse the transfer to Alaska that the Air Force was offering her and ask for a discharge.

"I feel disappointed in myself for not taking that transfer," she admitted. "I should have stayed in. How wrong I was to listen to Jim when a good career was staring me in the face!" Not many years later, her marriage ended on bad terms. He wasn't paying child support and fled to Texas. Her son told Diana where he was working, and state authorities took a monthly payment from his check from then on. Today, when he is around, he talks nonstop about the fun stuff they did when they were together, most of which Diana can't recall.

For decades, Diana worked for Walmart and retired several years ago. She has a good life filled with hobbies and relations with her grandchildren, who love her dearly.

CHAPTER 16:

Corner Lot Circus Carnies

D ad was renting the piece of property I mentioned previously, located close to the Causeway in the southeastern part of Tampa. The location placed us not too far from Copher's auto salvage yard near the center of a terribly unkempt yard containing a block house that sat in pieces. Broken blocks were somehow scattered throughout the inside of the structure, with a good bit of wrecked concrete portions surrounding it. Behind our trailer, a little distance east from a fence in utter disrepair was the entrance to one of the largest national Carnival crews. It housed the truck mechanics, the fellows who set up the tents, and the drivers who drove the caravan from town to town.

It was the winter, not too cold, just right for getting out of the house for a walk, which Doug and I did while I was visiting, having driven down from Neptune Beach.

"You want to walk with me to the carnie camp?" Doug asked. He sounded like he had a real treat ahead for me. I happily obliged.

I knew only what I'd heard about the circus and its acts. No face-to-face experience had I encountered, even though the worker bees from their large group lived close to Dad's place.

"Sure, I've got nothing to do." I was anticipating purely an introduction to the blue-collar workers who were the ones who kept the business alive. Those who made up the shows lived farther south, in Gibsonton, about a twenty-minute drive.

After a short walk, we stepped onto the property overseen by the laboring carnies, where I was introduced to one of Doug's friends, Rich, a mechanic who kept the trucks and other vehicles of the circus in top shape. The hood of a truck near where he stood was open, so I guessed it had to be the motor he was working on. Watching his hands, I saw he was removing the water pump.

"Here, let me help," I said. Changing a water pump I learned to do at an early age, back when cars were so much easier to repair. I picked up the wrench and assisted with the loosening of the bolts.

"You like the circus life much, Rich?" I asked. His hair reached below a ball cap that was turned around to keep the bill from getting in the way of his work. It had stains on it, which proved that the better part of his years with the circus was spent around engines. Grease lined the underside of his fingernails, and his tone was welcoming. Doug and he, as I could see and hear, were close friends.

"It's not a bad living. I never was much for book learning, so I did what most boys think at least once. I ran off to join the circus. Fixin' trucks came later once the boss found I caught on quick." A rag near him he picked up to wipe his hands and held out his right one to give me a handshake.

"It seems to suit you, this sort of work," Doug said." It's not like you're without your own space. Hell, look at this. The area is wide, and you have the financial support you need to purchase whatever tools you need." He collected scattered tools and set them in a pile on the rim of a gigantic tire meant for another truck.

Rich kept a busy schedule. "Plus, I must be on call. Whoever needs a hand, I must be available."

"I guess you've seen it all, haven't you?" I asked.

"Pretty much. Would I have rather done something else? No, not without more learning. The circus has its own culture in both how we live among one another and how we promote the stars of the sideshows. You know the conjoined twins, Ronnie and Donnie? They can't read or write. I heard none of the schools wanted them, and so they remain, to this day, untaught."

Amazing, I thought, how they lived their entire lives illiterate.

Ronnie and Donnie later died on July 4, 2020, of congestive heart failure at age sixty-eight, the oldest living conjoined twins in the world. I was surprised to learn that most surviving conjoined twins are females. Ronnie and Donnie enjoyed playing softball when they visited Gibtown, the nickname given to the town by carnies, and ran faster than I thought capable. Their hometown was Akron, Ohio, a mere hour-and-a-half drive from my birthplace in Rochester, PA. They were joined from the sternum to the groin and shared a set of organs. After a two-year stay in the hospital, it was determined they could not be safely separated.

I searched my mind, as, even in those days, I was a reader. The freaks, as I saw them, were poor souls. But are they overlooked by God? I recalled the strength of Samson that was in his hair and the man by the pool of Bethesda who barely moved when the waters troubled.

"Such a contrast. I just read about the hairy-faced fellow named Jo Jo. What was he called? The dog-faced boy? The literature stated he was well-learned, that he could speak five languages, and that his education was well past high school. So, the differences in freaks, I suppose, is big," said Rich.

My attention turned to our work when I heard Rich say, "I think the pump is about to free up. Here, let me reach in there." We pulled it off and put the new one on.

Over the next few weeks, I walked over to visit Rich again and again. We repaired a drive shaft after he allowed me to drive over to Cophers for the U-joints while we harped on circus talk. Surely, tired of reciting all the shows the circus contained, Rich, nevertheless, listed for me all the acts he could recall.

"There's the Grady Stiles family. You know them, the folks with the lobster-like hands. They lived here. Then there's the rubber-faced man, the monkey girl, and the conjoined Hilton sisters." He touched on the rumors that were going around regarding the Stiles family's criminal history. I wanted nothing to do with going on about that because I'd heard Grady Stiles wasn't a pleasant man to deal with.

During the town's heyday, its population included some of the most renowned sideshow acts in history.

Al, "The Giant" Tomiani, and his wife, Jeanie, "The Half-Woman" lived in Gibtown. They gave up the sideshow business to be self-employed. Al was a local politician.

"I think they're in town," Rich said. "You wanna go? You hungry, Dave, Denny? We can drive down to Al's diner to grab a bite to eat. It's not far. Less than twenty minutes." Doug was anxious to get a bite of Jeanie's tasty fries.

I turned to Denny, and he nodded. "Sure, let's go."

We were lucky to find Al at the restaurant because, as I learned, he held many positions for the Gibsonton community. His incredible business mind enabled him to increase his income beyond what he made in the circus. After buying the property, the Alafia River in Gibtown became an angler's paradise. Al knew how to advertise and thereby created a 'must stopover' for Florida travelers. It was one of the rarest of vacation spots. For Al, it became a means of self-employment, which earned him a release from circus circuits.

"You get awfully tired of being gawked at over the years," Al said, "And besides, so much of circus work is built on fabrication. I'm only seven-foot-four, not eight-foot-four."

As we drove up, Al was fiddling with a sign that began to lean. His height helped with the job. "We'll lend you a hand if you need us," I said.

"Yeah, sure," Al said. "Run to the back of the house and fetch me my saw. You'll see it on a table back there."

Denny ran after it while Rich and I stood near Al. He towered over our five-and-a-half feet stature. To new people, Al liked to talk about himself at his own pace and friendly way, confessing, at the same time, that he really disliked being an attraction. To be a friend was all he cared to be.

A good example was the Gibsonton owners, who proclaimed, billed, and featured Al Tomaini's physical dimensions. Was Al's shoe size truly twenty-seven and his weight 356 pounds? Only Al and his former promoter knew. Years passed as Al worked various circuses, including the Great Lakes Exposition in Chicago, which is where he met Jeanne Tomasini, known as "The Living Half Girl." She was born without legs and was a mere two feet, five inches tall, as advertisements stated. Promoters billed the two as "The World's Strangest Married Couple."

"Sorry if we seem to view you as someone odd, Al," I said as I came back with the saw. "You seem like just any other man to me, although I'm a kid, so I'll be impressed for a good while yet."

"Truth is, I'm uncomfortable being stared at all the time." It was his thyroid that gave him trouble and caused his physical demise; nothing he chose on his own.

"I apologize," Rich said. I was working on that big semi when Denny, Doug, and Dave came along. "I thought they might like to eat lunch here."

After those words, Al relaxed. He was such an affable guy. Easy-going to the extreme. A friendship with him seemed to manifest in seconds. He told us more about himself, then added, "You want Jeanne to fix you up a meal, go on in and let her know."

We chose cheeseburgers and fries and waited to be called inside. Al opened about his stats and responsibilities.

He told us he set up a trailer court, constructed a diner and a TV repair shop, and built "The Giant's Fishing Camp" on the grounds near the river, where we stood. In fact, those words on a large sign at the front of the premises announcing Al's domain remained for years after he passed. Humanitarian and compassionate, Al and Jeanne adopted five children, but at fifty years of age, Al died because of a pituitary tumor. It had given him trouble for years, which is what I must have been perceiving as we readjusted his outdoor sign.

Today, there remains only the Circus Museum to visit. There aren't any of the acts left living in Gibtown. About all that's left is the Museum maintained by the International Independent Showmen's Association, Inc., known to most as the "Gibtown Showmen's Club." They are a nonprofit private organization made up of people in the outdoor amusement industry.

The original club building opened in 1966 and has expanded to be the largest Showmen's Association in the United States. They have grown to over 4500 members from all over the United States and several foreign countries.

At its height, the grounds included a post office with a low counter for "little people." Siamese twins ran the fruit stand. Lions, elephants, and monkeys lived in backyard pens; carnival rides were parked in driveways all over town. Among the eye-catchers were the woman with a long black beard and the tall monster who married her. In addition, there was a man brought into this life with his head affixed to a body resembling a short, stout snake, like a large maggot, with a little length on him.

Al donated the first ambulance, became the president of the Chamber of Commerce, the fire chief, the designer and builder of the community hall, and the deputy sheriff, along with his little friend, Colonel Casper Balsam.

In reading about the town, I discovered that within the nation, Gibsonton was one of the few places that provided zoning to accommodate circus animals on residential property.

Questions and stares shown by busybodies wanted to know the means by which these odd individuals found purpose living in bodies that were so unnatural. "I guess you live with what God gave you," Ronnie once said.

Today, to the east side of Gibsonton, is where tourists pay twelve dollars to view the memorabilia of circuses and fairs. Inside that large yellow building is everything from carnival games such as dart and circle tossing to supposed skeletal remains of Siamese twins.

I later heard Ward Hall, the owner of the Gibsonton Showmen's Museum, say in an interview that he had hundreds of human oddities who worked at the circus, including giants, midgets, the alligator-skinned man, the tattooed lady, the bearded lady, the monkey girl, the living half-man, and dwarfs.

"They are the hardest working and most reliable people in the world you'd want to get along with," he said.

At age 88, Hall passed away in Sun City Center, Florida, on August thirty-first, 2021. I would perform with my band, EZ Street, on numerous occasions to entertain retirees, as well as ones who needed special care.

So successful the circus business had been, the Gibtown carnival contributed thousands of dollars to an assortment of charities because, as Hall said, "Carnival people are the most generous and loyal people you will find in your life. They know what hard work is, so they can appreciate people who need a lift.

"Many of my people are religious," Hall said. "They're Catholics, and, to serve believers, this carnival business had its own Vatican-ordained priest, Father John."

Ward believed the hard part was the setting up of the carnival. It could take all day to put up a ride, but when its over, workers have to take it down, drive maybe 200 miles to the next show location, and start the process all over again. They did this for eight to ten months per year. Hall bought up some competitors and was soon one of the dominant presenters in a shrinking field.

These days, the sideshows are no longer around. Their popularity was the highest in the forties and fifties. Surprisingly, even though Ward Hall bought into the business late, he made a good run of it, even while he slowly watched the carnie life breathe its last breath.

Understandably, the changing attitudes about physical differences led to the decline of the freak show. Such entertainment towards the end of the nineteenth century began to fade even then. It was time for science to take a turn. Progressive thought labeled these conditions as being genetic mutations or diseases, and freaks became the objects of sympathy rather than fear or disdain; thus, the carnie life ended.

If science has its way and all the *freaks* of this world are brought into the public, are seen walking the malls, or taking a swim at the beach, just how would the public react today? As I view it, I don't believe this world is ready for such intense diversity. The existence of evil, as I view it, is not on a decline in this universe but rather sliding into greater growth. The sort of compassion needed to bring these people into our lives comes only from the most kindly empathetic attitude heaven can impart to God-fearing people, and even those who profess godly allegiance will be put off, for the sanctification process the Holy Spirit desires to perform in the saints is slow and tedious, not an overnight work.

An hour passed, and we headed north to the truck lot. We talked about the assortment of acts while I helped to set in the water pump, tightened the bolts, and sneaked a sip of beer. Rich taught me about the use of exaggeration and overstatement. It was a major tool and played a big part in producing the desired reaction by audiences who thought they knew the actual from the fake.

CHAPTER 17:

Mom's Life

When I reflect on my dreadful past, shocking images of Mom's aim to end her life come to mind. Even after sixty years, I see I am very much controlled by that event.

I still do not know why Dad and Mom's marriage fell apart. My age blinded me to marital issues. I lacked discernment about what took place in our home. What led Mom to try to do away with herself? Did anyone understand her mental condition? Had she even seen a psychiatrist? Could Mom have cracked under the weight of cooking for a family of six, cleaning the basement, and taking care of us four kids and a husband?

Mom's act affected my brothers, sister, and me for years to come. Such an incident should have been plenty to endure for the lifetime of any person, but more traumas lay ahead. Another interruption occurred as I stood playing my bass in a Saint Petersburg fraternal organization.

My aunt in Pennsylvania had traced my band schedule to the club. She had important news to pass on. A believable story she told me. Mom had been in a car accident, and Denny and I should rush home. Unsettled, I felt fear as we packed our gear. Guitar and amplifier cords lay scattered on the stage, the common aftermath of every job. I tossed them into a large black bag without care. Speaker cables, I grabbed in a heap and tossed into an old suitcase. I suspected that Aunt Sis had not told the full truth.

As we began our road trip to Pennsylvania, the most horrific news of my life was forwarded by a second call that left me shattered and drained. Did Mom survive? Was she dead? The first bit of news presented by Sis, with an unexcited tone, was that Mom was a victim of a road accident and was presently a patient being treated at the Rochester General Hospital. We naturally assumed, by the lack of emotional distress in Sis' tone, that things would be all right, that Mom was in good hands, and her condition was hopeful.

Twenty years prior, Mom was placed in government housing located in Rochester, Pennsylvania following her release from the Dixmont State Hospital. Her tiny, three-room apartment was located three blocks up the side of a hill in Rochester, about a quarter mile west of the Bridgewater Bridge. On the heels of Mom's discharge from the asylum, the authorities had placed her in state government housing. I had visited her little apartment, reminiscent of a place of confinement. Light brown metal doors to each cramped residence clanged when in use. A few residents kept their doors ajar. I heard televisions penetrating the hallways broadcasting daytime soaps and game shows. It seemed more like a well-furnished cell than an apartment.

This complex rested on a hill built on leveled ground, which gave space for its construction. It can be a shock for one to visit such accommodations to see for themselves lives reduced to such bottom-of-the-line living standards.

Each time I visited Mom, she looked disheveled. It was how she grew to be while living in that place. Nothing fancy did she need. She was in an awful state, which caused me to despair.

"Do you need anything?" I'd ask, hoping to cheer her up. She'd shake her head and glance at me kindly despite the foggy veil the daily routine of consuming medications created. She enjoyed a sense of freedom as I helped her to my car. Each time I visited, I offered to drive her to the park, a favorite place for her, where she would sit on a wooden bench in a cool, shady spot, where a soft breeze existed. The change from her residence, caused her to come alive and soothed her. During quiet moments, she found enjoyment in the reading of a novel, or she would work on one of her spectacular doilies. Beautifully crafted completed ones filled her living room table spaces and bedroom.

A quiet, undisturbed attitude, with seldom a complaint, she showed on these getaways. Mom disliked a solitary existence and treasured the company of her kids and the few friends she made at mental health care functions. She lacked even a moderate income, for she possessed no more money than her absolute needs demanded to buy her necessities, and she asked for very little. The obvious traits she displayed, a special harmlessness and peacefulness, I envied. I looked at her as a true dove.

I'd stop by as often as my work would permit. Four jobs I held. I lived in the next town, New Brighton, with my wife, and sometimes slept on Mom's couch to give her company. She liked standing by the bathroom as I shaved, watching her son doing masculine maintenance. It gladdened her to have me by her.

One day, she asked me to cut her toenails. I agreed but regretted my offer when I looked at her disfigured nails. I identified the job as loathsome, but I pushed myself to do it, to make her realize her importance to me.

"Where are the nail clippers, Mom?" I asked.

"They're in that drawer, hon, over there." She pointed to a small chest at the foot of the bed. "Move stuff around. You'll find them." I knelt, lifted the top of the container, and shuffled through items as I searched for the clippers. I moved aside an eyeglass repair kit, hair brooch clips, safety pins, needles, an assortment of threads, a cassette tape, small knitting needles, fabric, a small portable radio, batteries, and candles until I found a large, rounded set of nail clippers.

"Here they are!" I spoke. Then I knelt in front of her and reached for her left foot. For a moment, I held the foot in my hand and stared at the thick, deformed toenails, realizing with a sinking sense that it was impossible to cut them in a normal fashion. The work demanded a professional with the proper tools.

"What does the podiatrist do, Mom?" I asked her. "I can't latch onto a piece to cut." How on earth was I going to do this? I asked myself. Unable to force the cutter deep enough to latch onto a piece of toenail, the care frustrated me. Snipping a small piece here and there was all I could do. My efforts ended with little success.

"There, Mom, that's the best I can do. You need a professional, not me," I told her. "You find the place, and I'll drive you, okay?" Had I known podiatrists were able to cut off toenails, as I have had done to mine, that would have been the answer to Mom's dilemma. She would never have to suffer the bending it required to reach her feet.

"Thanks, hon. I'll call around," she said, but she never got back to me. My visits were frequent, as I had rerouted my house stops for an extermination company I worked for. Sometimes I turned away from my planned schedule to check on Mom. They were brief visits only. Weekend afternoons and evenings, when booked, I spent fulfilling wedding music contracts with a four-piece band. On weekdays, following my stops at homes and businesses until 2:00 p.m., I either sorted books, built shelves for the bookstore, or covered stories for the local county newspaper.

Mom's four-pack of cigarettes per day habit was supported, in a large part, by Dad's supply to her. He smoked Pall Malls and Mom smoked Salems. If Dad didn't arrive to her house at three o'clock twice each month to drop off her supply of smokes for two weeks, she became very uncomfortable under the weight of her addiction.

My mother's persistent needs and demands drained her mother and older sister. Eventually, they stopped visiting her. This left her with me and my brother Denny (at least once a month) as her only visitors. I did as much as my time allowed, for she needed help. How did she get along without someone to step in?

How she lived in that complex was a mystery to me. I loathed Mom's government-monitored existence and wanted something better for her. Years later and married, I thought my wife and I should ask Mom to move in with us to an equally small apartment attached to our large town home.

"No way!" Mom protested. "They would take away my government benefits."

And so, she stayed thirty years in that god-forsaken shelter, a home for deeply challenged loners.

One day, having had her limit of an empty life, Mom walked Rochester's half-mile incline of walkways and roads to the railroad yard at the bottom level, located alongside the Ohio River.

Eight or nine tracks made up the yard. On these, Mom walked, seeming, at first, to head for a bench to sit and read along the water's edge.

A fast-moving train whose engineer spotted Mom walking on his set of tracks blasted his train whistle again and again. Onlookers standing on the upper-level bridge yelled in her direction. Convincingly planned, Mom kept to her agenda, never to take the first step off those tracks. Trackmen found her under the twelfth car before the train came to a halt.

That news produced in me intense sadness, overwhelming grief, and anxiety. Mom was only sixty-one years old. Why did she opt to end her life? Was loneliness her reasoning? Or perhaps, the fault lay with the refusal of her mother and sister to support her. The shock was unbearable. To a large extent, I blamed her offspring for leaving Mom by herself, alone in a world that was on a survival level, heartless, and full of limitations. Years earlier, I had moved out of state to improve and develop a broader journalism career, but after her death, I told myself my vision should have been as much about providing care for my mother as it was about getting ahead as a writer.

Even though I was within my options for a better life, I looked at myself as being selfish and unresponsive. Should not one's parents be a factor when choosing a course in life? She gave birth to me, loved me as much as any mother should, and still, the biggest part of her days expired unaccompanied. My mother lived in hell while I strove to build a career.

With the funeral over, my sister Diana and I, for two afternoons, cleaned Mom's apartment. We wanted it to shine when the state inspector came to repossess the property, so we scrubbed everything in sight: the floors, all kitchen surfaces, the refrigerator inside and out, the bathroom, and the single living room window. The corners of the floor and under furniture collected dust and dirt, and the windowsills, once the knick-knacks got wiped, were washed as well. We had no time or resources to paint anything, so we cleaned the walls.

I called Goodwill, offering them her bed, kitchen table and chairs, and sofa, which they accepted. They may have dumped them at the nearest landfill or kept a couple of pieces for themselves. Wherever released, either dropped off or disposed of, they were gone. All that remained were insignificant items, a torn and worn recliner, kitchen utensils, plates, pots and pans, a shower curtain, trash cans, an old broken sewing machine, wall displays, decades-old drapes, and ashtrays, all of which my sister and I loaded into a rented truck and unloaded at the dump.

I kept four wall ornaments, all coated with a conspicuous nicotine yellow stain: the Ten Commandments, a picture of Jesus holding a lamb and shepherd's staff, a parrot made by gluing colored rice onto a pattern drawn on wood, plus simple reminders of her existence, envelopes filled with dated photographs and a life insurance policy worth a mere $500, nothing more.

I remember an old manual typewriter sitting on the kitchen table, where Mom used to eat away an hour here and there typing text from newspapers and magazines she found in doctors' offices. It provided exercise for her arthritic fingers.

The next day, Diana and I returned to Mom's apartment to double check our work. We scrubbed the walls of the bathroom, giving special attention to the dark spots behind the base of the toilet. I had already tightened the loose towel rack with the few tools I had on hand when Dad walked through the door of the bathroom. Not showing the least bit of gratitude for the work Diana and I had done, he demanded I stop. "Do nothing until you find whatever paperwork your mother might have put away!" He repeated, "Did you hear me? Do nothing until you find whatever paperwork Doris might have put away!" He was annoyed by the irresponsibility he imagined he saw in me.

I dropped the sponge and grabbed a towel to dry my hands, fetched a box I found in Mom's bedroom, and emptied it on the floor. Among odds and ends, including newspaper clippings, her typings, and faded photographs of us kids in a child's plastic pool, I found her death benefits. It contained little of value.

"Find what she received from her mother's estate! Do it! She had to be given something," he said. "Now!" His harsh, uncaring comment showed he cared for nothing more than whatever money or item he could walk away with.

Dad continued. "Will you ever be a man? Will you ever grow up?"

Not once do I recall my father accepting me or talking to me from a father and son perspective, as he never, in his entire life, viewed me as having matured. Like most of the millwork, blue-collar fathers I knew, he maintained a distance and refused involvement in the upbringing of his children. Entirely unaware of the effect the lack of it had on the mental health of his children and wife, his refusal to change carried with it a lasting repulsion against authority, especially government agents.

I sensed a knot twist in my stomach and anger rose to the back of my throat. My pulse raced. How dare he speak to me in that manner? How dare he manipulate me and turn everything I did, including the good I accomplished, into a cynical statement. His manipulative temperament turned all of life gloomy and pessimistic. I spoke my mind. "Fuck you, fuck you, fuck you," I exploded. "Get out of this apartment now. Leave! Or I will call the police. You are only here wondering if there is something you can lift that's of value."

At that moment, I decided never to see my father again for the rest of my life. It was my form of punishment for his refusal to respond to grief, and it was all due to his redneck/hunky character, which my siblings and I suffered for years. He refused to view us as adults. Instead, being Mom's ex-husband, he told himself he had all the answers and pushed his way into matters that should not have pertained to him, including attempts to take whatever he thought belonged to him.

Years later, while in family dysfunction therapy, I stepped away to gain distance, which helped me to understand the influences that surrounded men out of the 50s-80s union culture. Perhaps from the hard work, heat, and limited education, the men adopted strong vulgarity, racism, brutality, alcoholism, and distorted, one-sided views. The talks in the mills daily were filled with black humor and mean-spirited wit, and fathers took this same culture home with them, transforming themselves, and their kin, into selfish, often unaffectionate, emotionally blocked despisers of those who well earned their financial success and high-level educations. Whether they were welders, carpenters, miners, laborers, steel workers, ironworkers, or men in chemical and glass factories, many of these union men adopted a deeply sarcastic culture and clung to it all their lives.

I hope to see a significant change take place within groups of men who associate day after day with one another, such as members within plants, mills, and foundries. There is indeed a culture that arises out of these industries that is rarely for the betterment of the workplace, community, and family. Sarcastic men must realize the kind of contributions they make to others around them when what they insist on conveying is a bigoted, jolly vulgarity that breeds nothing positive.

Planting in the hearts and minds of kids a stabilized culture benefits relations with all involved. It is not corny to think love, joy, peace, long-suffering, gentleness, meekness, temperance, and goodness should take the lead in attitudes and conversations, even in the most strength challenging toil. Mockery, ridicule, and satire can sometimes be funny, but those attitudes need to be judged for the damaging influence they have in creating a blue-collar, chauvinistic mentality.

I finally broke my promise to myself and visited Dad as he lay on his bed, about to take his last breath, wheezing and coughing because of painful emphysema.

CHAPTER 18:

Extra Duty

Following my high school graduation, I had enlisted in the Navy. Three and a half years later, my enlistment had expired. My discharge was given at my request. With only eight months left before the end of my commitment, my annual assessments were showing improvement. There was a reason for that. By then, I'd become a Christian. It certainly caught me off guard, my spiritual awakening, and it showed. My inward change was noticed by commissioned and non-commissioned shipmates alike.

No doubt, I experienced a very emotional transformation, but, by then, I had been, within the space of less than four years, dismissed from one division to another because I spoke the truth when wrong commands were thrown at me, none of which permitted me a word in defense.

Once, as I stood watch on the aft lookout, my replacement had not climbed the ladder to relieve me and the mess decks were about to shut down. I called to the lead petty officer on the bridge to please send someone to replace me, as my watch had elapsed fifteen minutes ago, and I was told to remain as I was, on aft lookout (while underway).

The chow line was only minutes from shutting down, and I was hungry and needed to visit the head. Angered by the command to remain on post, I told the E-4, "Either send someone to relieve me, or I will walk off." Which I did.

That action afforded me two weeks of extra duty grinding grit off the interior decks without ear protection. My annoyed overseer said he could find no protective earplugs for me. To this day, I continue to suffer from severe tinnitus (ringing ears), for which they awarded me a VA disability. The command's refusal to provide the proper safety equipment caused my disability for which the government pays me $149 each month. My hearing was damaged too, so I wear hearing aids, provided by the local VA hospital. Being close to the artillery during practice battle stations didn't help matters either.

Other idiotic instructions followed, each one taking away from me whatever they felt I had left to give, to where, after shifting from one division to another, I ended up below decks, classified as the lowest level boiler tech fireman. My final assignment had me below decks to work as a boiler tech. I didn't mind the work so much as I did the go-fer position, they gave me. Anything wanted above decks was my duty to retrieve it, even if it was nothing more than a bucket of iced tea.

When I asked the ship's commander for a discharge, he gave me one under general conditions. The stipulation required I promise to give the captain guitar lessons, one every afternoon at 2:00 p.m., to which I consented. After our talks, I could see that he understood my position, admitting the ship had a lot of shipmates with problems that needed to be addressed. My hopping around from one division to another was not entirely my fault, he admitted. The ship's crew possessed some real challenges.

He knew I was a very good watchman, having sited many ships out at sea long before radar picked them up on their screens. Also, I steered the helm well in some of the worst seas on the globe, i.e., around the Cape of Good Hope. Prior to working below decks, I was assigned to the laundry, or, as the service was known, ship's service. While a laundryman, I cleaned and pressed the uniforms of all officers and worked long, boiling hours while docked in the hottest African ports in the Middle East. As the ship's personal mess cook for the Chiefs, I endured some of the worst attitudes imaginable from self-important lifers who had little to no ability to work civilian jobs. Many of them knew not how to be pleasant or thankful, merely bossy.

CHAPTER 19:

Jail time, Missed Ship's Movement

I was driving down the long dirt driveway that led to my off-base rental, not noticing anything, just thinking about cleaning up and making a burger. That's when a police car began to follow me. I wondered why he was behind me and soon found out.

My brother had asked me if I would put up three of his friends he met at a concert "until a check arrived" for them in the mail. I obliged even though I knew not one of them. What could possibly go wrong?

Those bums were three wandering long-hairs: one sixteen-year-old girl, an early twenties fellow, and a thirty-something man who told Denny all they needed was a place to stay for three days. The house I was renting off base was located about five miles from the naval station in the middle of a copse of woods. A long dirt road led to my yard and front door. A chain link fence surrounded the quarter-acre lot. The house was nothing special, just a place to unload after a day's work aboard the destroyer, the USS Noa (DD-841).

Little did I know, these three itinerant wanderers were packing some highly illegal items. I'd find out the hard way. As my car approached the house, behind me, I noticed the police cruiser pulling into my yard. He had no colored lights on, so I thought his business had nothing to do with mine.

Maybe some sort of county work would be getting underway in a few days. Who could know? After all, I was living in the woods. Boy was I mistaken.

I put my '64 Chevy II in neutral and pulled up the emergency brake. Noticing a police officer walking toward me, I was ready to politely greet him. He beat me to it. "What's your name?" he asked like he'd said those words a hundred times before. I watched his hands reach for something. I thought it would be a pad, but it turned out to be a set of handcuffs. He didn't use them right away.

"Do you have any ID on you?" he asked.

"What's this all about, officer? I just got off a long, hard day cleaning boilers," I said as I reached for my billfold in my right rear pocket. I browsed through it to find my driver's license and Navy ID. He took them. I noticed a scar on his left cheek that fit a policeman's profile.

"Are you renting this property?" His eyes looked over my house and yard. I cut the grass the past weekend and trimmed the shrubs. The place looked good.

"Yes, sir. My brother asked if I would allow a few friends he met at a concert the other night to stay with me until a check arrived for them in three days." Sweat poured from my forehead down to my wrists as the officer placed the cuffs on me.

"Because your name is on the lease, we must place you under arrest for causing illegal disturbances and for the drug paraphernalia that we found outside and inside your home. Neighbors reported hearing some shooting near your house. When we got here, we found three people shooting a handgun in the backyard. They've been hauled off. We then inspected your house. There's been marijuana found growing in pots on your roof, and the house contained drug syringes and containers we will be analyzing. Plus, this girl is only sixteen, so we also have you contributing to the delinquency of a minor. Follow me."

He led me to his police cruiser, opened the rear door, and kept me from hitting my head as I ducked to get inside. I was unloaded at the Jacksonville County jail where lots of paperwork was filled out. I wondered what would happen to me once the Navy Shore Patrol came visiting. I would soon know. After two days, two tall SPs called me downstairs and led me into a private room. Immediately they grabbed me and shoved me against the wall. They both hit me in the gut and slapped me hard against the back of my head. I was such a tiny fellow. Were they going to really hurt me or just scare me?

They wanted to know how involved I was in illegal drugs, and I told them that I had no knowledge of any of it. I didn't smoke, inject, or swallow any of that stuff. They obviously were assigned to frighten me, to force me to be submissive. But to what? I had nothing to tell them. All I did that day was go to work and head back to the house.

Before the SPs left, I could tell they wanted to keep me locked up for as long as the Navy was willing to show me who's boss. My only alternative was to call my father. I told him the truth about what happened, and with his sort of former Navy brig attitude, accepted I was locked up. After all, it had happened plenty of times to him when he was enlisted. To my surprise, he sold his boat floating in the Crystal River lagoon to get the bail money I needed. By then, I'd been living in a cell for eight long days. The worst part was the fact that the ship got underway while I was incarcerated, so I missed "ship's movement." It headed off to Gitmo, Cuba, to practice war games.

I remained in that cell with four other men with bunk beds and a TV, feeling more nervous than I'd felt in years. Getting along with the others, thankfully, was easy. Not one of them was a rough guy, but rather displayed a sort of kindness I thought was impossible to find in a jail. The older man, Red, quickly adopted me. His manner reminded me of those men I watched on film, who ran liquor in the 20s. We talked a good bit about our upbringing and various experiences, and he taught me a couple of card tricks that I do to this day.

.Dad drove me back to the Mayport Naval Base where I was assigned temporarily to the USS Yellowstone, a tender that seldom left the dock. I was told to wait while air travel aboard a cargo plane was secured. After another day, I was told to rush to the airstrip to board a huge plane that seemed like boarding an apartment. First, the pilot was to load at Norfolk, Virginia, then head south to Gitmo Cuba to unload. It was there that I would be returned to the Noa.

About a week later, a friend aboard the ship, Don "Yukon" Tanner, had shared the gospel of Jesus Christ with me. I knew I had found the answer among those who also understood what it was like to come out of a family of lost, lonely and unsettled souls.

His talk led me to a late-night confession of my sins, or as it was being labeled, rebirth. It certainly was exciting, and the work it did to my spirit brought a great sense of freedom. Without a doubt, change took place. I felt unburdened and, to a degree, carried less worries and heaviness on my shoulders. There was excitement to the point where I became evangelistic and led others to the Lord.

War games had us deployed to the port side of an aircraft carrier, perhaps one nautical mile away. Our duties as boatswain's mates on four-hour watches was to man the flight deck and with binoculars, search for aircraft and civilian vessels. All day shifts rotated BM seamen from the bridge to the flight deck. Once relieved, sleep came to me in seconds.

It was while we were cruising slowly without any particular mission that I noticed the Commander walking on the port side deck. Not caring what he might think, since I felt I'd grown to know him through so many Captain's Masts, I walked up to him to ask a question that I knew was time to admit.

"Sir, Commander, I wonder if I can ask something of you?"

"Sure, what's on your mind, seaman?"

"A few days ago, I was returned to the Noa after spending eight days in the Jacksonville County jail for doing nothing wrong. I was simply one big mistake, and still, I get back here and am placed on more extra duty. You know how often I've been given extra duty for situations I knew inside me were wrong. Not being relieved on after lookout when the chow line was about to shut down and I desperately needed to use the head? I had to leave my post. What other choice was there?

"And then there's the nearly eight months I worked as a mess cook instead of the usual three, followed by the time I slugged a third class for tossing out all of my locker gear when I had to rush to the head to wash out my bleeding mouth caused by dental work the previous day. He noticed my unlocked locker and thought I needed a lesson.

"I have only another eight months left to complete my enlistment, and as far as I can see, nothing about this Navy is going to change for me. Would you please consider setting me free to pursue a new career course? I'm getting nowhere on this boat."

"Have you thought much about what you might do for work?" This led to an extended discussion regarding the actual benefits of becoming a lifer. They sounded great in the long run, but if I was to stay, all I'd have was what presently faced me.

"This ship will not last much longer," he said. "In another year, everyone onboard will get transferred to other ships. You'll get re-stationed to another vessel, one that has a lot less hassle than this one. Won't you try it? At least one more hitch?"

"I want to enter college to earn a degree in music."

"I've watched you and your brother play. You're good. Do you think that will be enough to make a living?"

"I'm not sure where performance will lead me, but at least I will study something I love and perhaps change majors once something jumps out at me."

In less than two weeks, I was on the road heading for my father's latest place of residency in Homosassa Springs, Florida. That night, the Christian men at the Jesus House, located on the beach, let me stay until morning. An apple for breakfast set me back on the road headed south. I had nowhere else to go.

Dad was still living with Lou and ten-year-old Doug in a small trailer court when I hitchhiked to see him in Homosassa Springs.

I would, later in life, regret that I left the Navy. There was security in the military, plenty to eat, a bunk in which to sleep, a handful of close shipmates, and ship service men to do the laundry. I loved the beauty of the seas and sky as we cruised in the middle of the Atlantic. For over three years, the military offered more than just a new home. It provided a way to get out of a house where my stepmother smashed kitchenware on my father's head.

I decided to head for Dad's place as my intention was to purchase a vehicle with the $1200 in savings bonds I had stowed in my duffle bag. It was a 1962 Ford Econoline that took my attention, which I bought from a private owner. Dad was kind enough to line the van with an electric cable to allow me the convenience of plugging into an electrical source. The gesture was extremely welcomed a month later while I was driving to California. Unfortunately, I never got there due to breaking down. The drive shaft broke.

To get to Homosassa Springs, I partly hitchhiked and partly rode a bus from the Mayport Naval Station, my home port that lasted for over three years, located near Jacksonville, Florida.

Arriving at night, I was poorly welcomed. I knocked on a little eight-by-thirty-five-foot trailer door. It opened, and immediately I could sense that same ugly tension that had filled my existence wherever we'd lived. It was obvious to me they were still drinking and beating on one another. I could sense it in the air.

What a shock to be greeted like I was an insurance salesman. Not so much as a hug was offered in greeting. Instead, Dad held out a hand, offering to shake mine.

"Still the same crap going on, isn't it?" I snapped. "When is all this going to stop?"

The love I received from my father was seldom shown in words. His ability to express affection was limited, like so many of the other "mill hunkies" that saturated Southwestern Pennsylvania.

I pleaded for an answer, "Why do you never tell me that you love me? In all those years living with you, I never heard it once said to me."

"I thought I made that plain by working and bringing home a check that afforded groceries, and I fixed things that broke down," he replied.

"It is so obvious to me that you don't honestly feel anything for me. Do you love me, truly love me, or have you been purposely avoiding the words?" I questioned with great doubt, adding that I couldn't recall from him the first time he hugged me.

He changed the subject to one that, for months, obsessed him. He told me he was working on a way to get Lou out of his life, even if it meant feeding her illegal drugs. In fact, he asked me if I was able to acquire some acid. My brother, in later years, told me he was able to easily acquire a tab of acid and accommodated Dad's intent to force a show of insanity while sitting in a club. Obviously, it didn't work. She felt nothing.

Any day was a reason for Lou to drink. Holidays were merely an excuse to ramp it up a notch, which led to fighting. On the days that Dad and Lou fought, lashing out at one another for meaningless reasons, I felt bad for Doug. After Denny and I enlisted in the Navy, Diana was commanded by Lou to leave the house on the day she graduated from high school. Her choice was the Air Force. She shares her experience in the chapter I wrote on her.

Regrettably, Doug would be stuck, alone, with those two immature nutcases. Alone in that madness, he felt abandoned, and frequently cried. I too was distraught by condemnation, worried about him to no end. For him, I sensed it could be the end. Lou might actually shoot him. I was powerless to do anything for him. The feelings would triple in quantity as days, weeks, months, and years passed when my mind fell upon little Doug's plight. I wanted him to escape, just as we did, but his youth was a hindrance. After one day's fighting, Doug decided to abandon their home and live wherever it was quiet.

He learned to live under bridges and vacant housing properties. When up north, to cool his milk in the winter without electricity and a refrigerator, he constructed a wooden box that he attached to the window outside of his vacant, dilapidated shack. Dad knew where he was staying and would drop by to give him money to get by.

CHAPTER 20:

Living with the Church Community

F ollowing my discharge, I didn't want to return to Pennsylvania because of the winter chill, so I searched for an apartment to share with a Christian brother. A shoe salesman, Fred Delaware, let me rent the second bedroom in his apartment in Neptune Beach, where I stayed for just over a year. Six residences followed that move for various reasons.

In this case, Fred was the son of a well-to-do father, the owner of a prosperous Northeastern corporation which added to his general financial comfort. Cheques arrived through snail mail in various amounts to assist him with living expenses, while I was left to my own devices to pay for and attend college classes by working at whatever construction job opened to me.

For one Christian man, the owner of a roofing company, I learned to hammer in shakes and shingles for a pittance wage. The weight of a bundle of shingles I carried up a ladder with the shingles on my right shoulder. I weighed barely 130 lbs. at the time. All this work made me feel like a Jewish slave building Egyptian palaces. Complete exhaustion and a twisted shoulder were my only end, and this occurred day after day. A system of steps we made by nailing in boards to shelf-like attachments that stretched for eight to ten feet onto the most angular roofs aided in hammering in shakes or wood shingles. When less sloped, we duck-walked and scooted bundles as we progressed from section to section nailing in one shingle at a time. We laid each shingle individually side-by-side along their centered notches and aligned them to the chalk lines we snapped to keep the rows straight.

Despite great effort, my infrequent sidelining, which also included working as the University's Student Government Secretary, I stayed poor while I tried to complete my education. All my efforts failed to provide a secure financial status. Fred grew increasingly angry with me for being late on a monthly rent of $125. He had to know that I had school costs to pay. The GI Bill sent me almost nothing, a check each month for a meager $220. Finally, Fred threw me out.

To my luck, I quickly found a new home. I moved into an apartment in Atlantic Beach with another brother, Jeff. I'd just gotten to know him at a house meeting. While eating pizza one night in the kitchen, I asked him, "What are those check marks you make on the calendar?"

They weren't easy to miss as the chart hung on the living room wall near the off-white punch-button telephone.

He looked a little stunned by my inquiry. An inward debate gave way to hesitancy. Should he truthfully answer? "They are the days when I masturbate. I'm trying to stop. It's not easy." This admission was followed by an explanation of his past during his years in the Navy, as he too was a Navy veteran who found Christ shortly before he was discharged.

"I was actively involved with a group of other sailors from the ship I was on. We fooled around with one another in various apartments along the beach. God is working to deliver me from that urge."

His confession took me a little time to take in. Is he gay? I asked myself. We were taught to turn from such urges, which my roommate was striving to accomplish. I gave him a great deal of respect for his dedication.

"Are you experiencing condemnation?" I asked in a caring tone. "Boys in my hometown neighborhood used to fool around in barns with one another, even before they were able to get off. It was pure curiosity. I'm sure that was how it was with you; just being curious."

I assured him that there was not a single brother in the church who wasn't presently faced with his own issues regarding masturbation and sexual issues in general. After all, the Bible instructs all believers to flee youthful lusts. This was written for all men to heed, even those who were just awakening to their sexual urges. Some of the young men thought they were the only ones with sex drives and customarily kept their activities closeted.

I never did find out if my roommate thought of himself as being gay, although, throughout the following years I knew him, he never once dated, nor did he talk about women. For the other guys, in response to a newly added woman to the flock, especially one with a striking appearance, she became a target, to the point where some of the strongest and more aggressive brothers in the church challenged the others, "Leave her alone or face me." This was especially true during the earliest days of the Jesus Movement as pairings began to take place.

I asked my friend, "Who are you attracted to?" My question irritated him. Discussions with straight men in the church community introduced me to the existence of struggling gays in various groups. I was told there were gays as well as adulterers within various flocks. I suppose none of this should have been news to me, for men and women both are attracted to whoever they choose.

Plus, one of the most well-studied Bible teachers turned from his calling, returned to the university to earn a doctorate, and forsook the church without ever looking back. He later announced, by mail, to the community of believers that knew him best that he had his fill of the Christian life and Bible teaching. He had chosen to live an openly gay life as a professional as opposed to remaining a teaching minister.

It seldom took long before marriages were arranged. Some of those quick-pick attachments have lasted for nearly fifty years. For others, the realization of their mistakes took a few years to acquire, even when a child was involved.

CHAPTER 21:

Dallas

After I spent about two weeks with Dad, Lou, and Doug in Homosassa Springs, I decided I should drive to where I last heard Denny was living, in Dallas, TX. The heat of that state was almost unendurable. I thought Florida was bad. Dallas was an unbelievable hothouse.

I got the address of Denny's residence from an envelope. The days prior to GPS demanded directions be acquired from maps freely offered to travelers by gas station attendants. It took me, step by step, inch by inch, until I found the right apartment complex.

A friend of Denny's, Henry, was living alone in the apartment when I arrived, and he said he was waiting for Denny to return from a trip he'd taken hitching rides west.

Two weeks passed until Denny arrived at the apartment. Filthy from head to toe, the first thing he chose to do was to hop in the shower and toss all of his filthy clothes on the floor. Once cleaned, he walked out to the living room looking a bit more human than he had when he first arrived.

He had lots of stories to share about his road adventures. The invitation he regretted most was, once, while standing along an Idaho highway, a lady picked him up, took him to her house, and asked him if he would live with her. She wanted him to stay around in a bad way. There was plenty of work that needed to be done on her ranch.

"There's no telling what I could have turned out to be. I was so stupid for not taking her up on her offer," Denny told me later. "She fed me like a king. Her house had the hottest water in the world. I lay on the couch, where I immediately fell asleep and woke up to the most wonderful meal.

"She said there is no reason for me to wander around and go nowhere, and she was right." And yet, Denny chose to move on from Idaho to Wichita, where he met a couple of girls who sort of adopted him.

"They liked me," he said. "I didn't stay long, just got back on the road, headed for home."

A ride from Wichita, provided for him by a kind, friendly man, carried him over 1,300 miles, straight to his apartment in Dallas. Once the man learned Denny was a Vietnam Era Veteran, a special goodness emerged from his heart.

And so, out of the blue, he came walking into the apartment after I had spent a couple of weeks with Henry. While on the road, often getting no one to stop, Denny had slept anywhere he could find a spot alongside the road, even in cattle grazing lands. A bed was a welcome sight.

The next day, I returned to seeking employment. I called businesses all over Dallas in search of work to earn the money needed to repair my van's drive shaft. A group in need of furniture movers asked for Denny and me to help them. For two days, we barely managed the drudgery.

"A lot has taken place since we parted, when you left the Navy, and I was still onboard doing a second cruise," I said. "I had no clue where you were headed once you walked down the pier. My guess was either a friend in another state or Dad's place in Ohio. Anyway, you landed here. You're back. It's good to see you."

While in Dallas, I shared with Denny that I was now a Christian and persuaded him to attend a church with me. By blindly pulling out the yellow pages and pointing to a church name, we ended up becoming members of a UPC (United Pentecostal Church) group. Doctrinally, they are not sound, as they don't believe in the Trinity among other things, but we didn't know any better, and we were thankful for discovering a group of welcoming friends.

The money we made at day labor hauling furniture was able to put my van on the road. Much to my surprise, a couple of friends from Florida showed up, Scott Ogden and Denny Nelson, and with them aboard my van, we drove to San Antonio, Texas. Denny Nelson needed to see his Dad to discuss something important that we weren't let in on. During one of those days there, we walked across the border into Laredo, Mexico. I wasn't impressed by it and later discovered tourists should avoid this city. Drug cartels and weak police activity in the city made the city unsafe for travelers.

By the time we arrived in San Antonio, the van was kicking and bucking again, badly. The drive shaft wasn't properly repaired and balanced. Still, we used it to get us back to Florida, driving 45 MPH on I-10.

CHAPTER 22:

On Christian Living

O nce back at the beach, I searched for a place of fellowship and fell among a group of very innocent, zealous, not well-taught, yet happy, Jesus-loving, sandal-wearing, former hippies. Many were new to the Lord, while others had believed for perhaps a couple of years. In a large home along the shoreline of Jacksonville Beach, we met as often as a gathering formed.

We sang songs whose lyrics came straight from the Scriptures, raised our hands in praise, and, if there was room, danced with joy. Then, a message was given by one of four or so "older" brothers in the Lord whose teaching material came from the cassette tapes of leading charismatic voices on the airwaves. Mostly, it was all about getting one's needs met, and boy, did I have a bag full of needs stored in my mind.

Strange-sounding utterances emerged from the group as we worshiped and continued long past any understanding. Later that evening, I asked one of the brothers what that singing without words was all about. He explained, pointing in Scriptures, various text verses that mentioned something called tongues and spiritual songs.

As an example: 1 Corinthians 14:2, "For he that speaketh in an unknown tongue speaketh not unto men, but unto God: for no man understandeth him; howbeit in the spirit he speaketh mysteries."

Did I want that gift as well? I was asked. Absolutely, I did. So, we prayed together and without effort, I began to speak in tongues giving praise to the Lord and building myself up in my faith. It brought a most incredible inward filling.

I became one of the many Christian brothers who gathered with young men and women in various homes and storefront businesses. What made up my life was immersed in all things Charismatic, which caused me to become religiously preoccupied. Everything I thought about, I began to vet through religious screening. Associations with believers represented a family and, to a small degree, served as one.

In no time at all, men rose from among believers who gathered together in assorted homes and buildings along the Jacksonville beaches and proclaimed themselves leaders. I easily adopted all that I heard, what was contained in most sermons spoken by different men in different groups, but I wasn't yet a true student of the Scriptures, merely a reader. Keep in mind, I sought a family, and I thought this was it. For the most part, contents of the messages presented in innumerable meetings were the same, no matter where one attended.

Leading voices kept saying the gospel was all about getting one's needs met through a methodical pattern of prayer. This belief system emerged and struck the beach area through men who formed the Word of Faith or WOF movement: Kenneth Copeland, Oral Roberts, Creflo Dollar, E.W. Kenyon and the originator himself, New Thought philosopher Phineas Quimby, just to name a few. If what was asked of God didn't manifest, it was always the fault of the one in need. That person lacked sufficient faith, which is the core of the WOF movement, using one's faith to acquire anything but inward change.

Whatever was said by the older men who passed themselves off as leaders in Jacksonville was nothing more than the regurgitation of sermons, they memorized from teachers like the men I listed who bound themselves to a kind of spiritual conspiracy, initially without any more intent than to exhort believers. Later, as the number of newly saved and unstudied people increased, their target quickly altered to wealth building through tithes and offerings, and sales of various materials.

Plus, promises were made. To anyone who would give, they would get a greatly restored increase, up to one hundred times the amount of one's donation. Their promise also included healings, if one had enough faith, which was always the excuse when one's prayers were not answered. "Sorry, brother, you don't have the faith to receive." Their material was not deeply rooted in massive proof of materialized healings, certainly not when it came to the most serious forms of health issues.

In my earliest days, I tried to keep whatever constituted truth and God's guidance, but I was very prone to lean in the direction the ball was bouncing from season to season and revelation to revelation. After some years passed, the Shepherding Movement hit town. It was now time for all of us to seek a pastor to rule over us. Within the church, deviations gave birth to variations of truthful aspects that surrounded what it meant to live a Charismatic life. These deviations, over the years, promoted, and continue to promote, an assortment of emotionally charged, extremist, biblically one-sided or non-supported views.

The way the switch in belief patterns evolved operated like so: once I became a regular at one group after I listened to whatever repeated "truth" was spoken by an esteemed "father in the faith," then, soon afterward, perhaps a year or more, another marvelous "revelation" would come down the pike to shake up the crowds, then another revelation arrived within the space of numerous decades, all of which originated from a kind of "insider trading" with God.

None of what was taught to me for nearly six years of my Christian life was based on the first principles listed in Hebrews 6. Nothing was pointed out to me as having been birthed out of the need to learn and apply Scripture for the sole purpose of sanctification or inward change. It took me eight years of bouncing from one philosophical leaning to another before I discovered the study of the first principles was to lead me into the second work of salvation, sanctification. Before true study came along, throughout all those years, I never was shown what was meant by "sound doctrine."

There was little expressed to encourage the innocent to grow in knowledge or to dig deep into the Word in search of the whole counsel of God. What did exist, however, was what I learned to term, "steer messages," meaning the sermon contained a point here and a point there, with a lot of bull in the middle. Why? Because it was all about experiencing miracles and emotional highs rather than building a strong foundation in sound doctrine. It's easy to see why, because no one knew profoundly the principles of God found in Scripture.

My desire to maintain the formulas devised by the WOF and Shepherding leaders collapsed once the Bible came alive to me. If miracles were all that God was about, then why aren't WOF preachers visiting American veterans at their local VA? I worked in one for thirty years and witnessed not one of these WOF wolves restore the bodies of a single limbless soldier. So, I'm no longer chasing dreams. These days, I let God be God. I let His sovereignty rule.

Today's Charismatic leadership is pushing onto the understudied the need to exalt sessions of feelings over the pattern of growth established in Scripture, to take Jesus' yoke upon them and learn of Him. In no way does the Bible confirm emotion to override Bible truths, and yet that is exactly what is taking place in these present-day New Apostolic Reformation movements tied in with another movement, called Impartation.

Great disillusionment hit the Charismatic world after so many promises had failed to produce any solid manifestations of power. This is when what has become known as Grace churches emerged. They fill up principally with former hardcore Charismatic Christians who burned out on all the unfulfilled promises, leadership failings, and overwhelming disillusionment.

Another disappointment had been the way the leadership within Charismatic groups attach themselves to philosophies they contend God spoke to them – rather than them proving in Scripture what they put forward. Revelations became the norm. Today's emotional obsession cannot be proven through Scripture. All of those side roads, most of which are unbiblical and therefore error-driven and misleading, have been going on for decades and have caused more questions than answers.

Most of the time, the cause of disillusionment and loss of hope is starvation, not being properly fed the Word of God. I encourage the reader to forget the seeking of feelings.

I don't want what I write here to sound entirely like the product of some disgruntled believer whose reflections on his five decades of being a Christian are steeped with having spent only wasted time while I lived among various groups within the body of Christ. At the same time, I do want to express the reality of what one faces placing his or her spiritual growth in the hands of philosophies spouted by the WOF pack, including men like Kenneth Copeland, Kenneth Hagin, Joyce Meyer, Oral and Richard Roberts, Benny Hinn and Creflo Dollar, just to name a few.

First off, I know why I am to attend a church assembly: to connect with God, to find a deeper meaning to my life, to feel the peace of God, to strengthen spiritually, and to become a part of a community. That is the hope that all believers have even when they attend gatherings of various doctrinal persuasions. But one must be aware, for many philosophical and religious leanings are much like minefields.

I began my Christian life with barely a dime in my pocket. I could not give financially, as my dedication to complete my college education came first. It had to, because I had very little money coming in, even while I worked sideline jobs.

The truth is, my lack of funds did not sit well with leadership within the majority of gathering places. Consequently, they looked at me as being subpar, substandard. I was poor and although the Bible says, "The poor you have always with you," most of those in charge discouraged the addition of more and more low-wage members. I had barely a few dollars to give at any one time and could only offer my talent as a musician. To their minds, I was unable to tithe or give at a reasonably acceptable pace, and so I was, pretty much, set aside, left unnoticed, unwelcomed in the cliques made up of high-level leadership.

Did I have Christian friends? Without a doubt. Most of what we enjoyed laughing about was the ridiculousness of the life we were leading. Was what we were being told ever to manifest among us? Was it to come to pass, or were we hoping against hope? Thus, hilarious imitations of the leading preachers sprang up among us. And how funny they were! Worthy of a professional act!

The oldest and strongest cliques, in whatever group I attempted to belong to, never once offered the first handshake as I walked into the door toting my string bass. Several of those men held successful secular positions and cared very little that I existed. Instead of getting to know me, I was habitually set aside and left to myself without their friendship. So, many of the larger churches weren't like home at all to me. They never would be. The smaller ones kept the humor going so as to keep away discouragement. Perhaps this is why, today, I prefer home groups over organized religious services.

In small home groups, I made a few friends and enjoyed the company. Once I joined a more sizable assembly, I was just a number, another face, or a poor brother who had nothing to offer, essentially a nobody. Groups with a goodly number of members always ended up forming factions and creating within the assembly a kind of pecking order. They combined in cliques most with themes that represented their commonalities, such as financial status, sports, and travel. I fit in none of them, being that I could not afford more than the air to breathe, and so I was seldom greeted as I walked into a big group.

The messages that were being shared by these men of God, behind a mixture of podiums, seemed to resonate like spiritual truths, and so they were taken as such by those, like me, who took it for granted these men heard God speak to them, as they claimed constantly. I'm reminded of the following passage from the book of Acts. During the time the First Church was being constructed, lots of this adoption of unsound doctrine took place. That former condition of the Corinthian church is a token of what it was like as I found myself tickled by all the newest crazes floating throughout unaccountable churches.

Acts 17:20, "For thou bringest certain strange things to our ears: we would know therefore what these things mean. (For all the Athenians and strangers which were there spent their time in nothing else, but either to tell, or to hear some new thing)."

I was guilty of doing this very thing, "spent my time in nothing else, but either to tell, or to hear some new thing," but for me, it related mostly to how I might manage to convince God that I was worthy of good health, that I had earned it by my attendance, my sharing of the gospel, by giving of my bass playing for worship, and I confessed all the right Scriptures as I fought the devil off. . A concentration on sanctification would have prospered me more spiritually than the seeking of emotional rushes minus Scriptural doctrine.

Later, I would watch on YouTube believers like Nicholas James Vujicic, a forty-year-old Australian American Christian evangelist and motivational speaker of Serbian descent, who was born with tetra-amelia syndrome, a rare disorder characterized by the absence of arms and legs. How God has used that man is an amazing example of what the least of us can accomplish when we are properly trained in God's Word.

Some of the most pitiful victims of poor health I met while employed at the VA hospital were those who had to endure, for the remainder of their lives, the loss of limbs or other major deprivation. They never got visits from ministers who believed in miraculous and instant healings by prayer and the laying on of hands because the state of such patients is far removed from the splinters and twisted ankles they pray for in their churches. A visit to a VA spinal injury unit is another situation entirely. Equally as challenging would be the major psychiatric misery found in mental health wards.

Chasing the devil, blaming him for every discomfort life brings and God allows, is a sign of hyper spiritualism. I recall watching Copeland on a YouTube video rebuke the spirit of covid, saying he had commanded it to die and flee from the country. So, he was the originator of this dreadful curse, the devil? One day all that demon chasing will be laid aside for a strong acceptance of God's sovereignty. God allows much more than Charismatics are willing to accept and the proof is in their leading bookseller list which contains a large number of books on demonology.

Outside all those WOF saturated meetings, I had few friends, mostly the roommate with whom I shared an apartment, and a couple of good, close clowns, Dan Pauly and Richard Bailey, who ran a leather shop below my apartment. Richard would imitate the personalities of the men in church leadership like a professional on the Ed Sullivan show, and, in fact, he could impersonate Sullivan to a tee. His brand of comedy was like medicine to me. It broke up the seriousness of the prevailing church politics. How I miss his company. He passed away on February 19, 2019.

A nice break from the doctrinal disputes was when four of us musicians drew together to form a Christian band called Selah. I found places for us to perform for free including a college campus, malls, and coffee houses. That lasted a couple of years and broke up when the female lead decided to get married.

Later, after hopping from one Charismatic group to another and allowing myself to remain vulnerable to whatever extremist revelation came down the Charismatic pike, I dropped out of attending altogether.

I needed something but had no clue what it was. There was more than what I had been brainwashed into clinging to, and it was impossible to obtain it from any of the existing Charismatic extremes. The evangelical community gained my ear through many very sound teachings, even though they do not include the acceptance of the Pentecostal experience. In fact, it was their sermons and first principal teachings that brought me deliverance from chasing emotion filled services void of strong teachings on sanctification.

One of the brothers who felt like me told me about a group of Christians who attended daily bible studies in a rented daycare center and occasionally went swimming together. I attended day and night classes with them for at least a year and a half. As I wrote, small groups are best for me. I was delighted to have found actual Biblical training in which I excelled under the tutelage of a very gifted young man, Mike Westbury.

The training left time on Sundays to research the notes from the previous week. It was a rule I took to heart, to not believe anything until I uncovered confirmation in the Scriptures. Not doing so was a major fault within my previous approach to Bible reading and haphazard study. It left me defenseless against whatever was being made up by leaders who either mimicked the last teaching they heard or who wanted to appear as if God "spoke" to them personally. It kept me from continuing the pattern of taking in, hook, line, and sinker, whatever was spoken to me by older men, without searching the Scriptures to see if what I was hearing was so.

Acts 17:11, "These were more noble than those in Thessalonica, in that they received the word with all readiness of mind, and searched the scriptures daily, whether those things were so."

When it came to church attendance or meetings, I'd had enough. Walking into a meeting every time the doors were open grew to be an obsession that I had to erase from my thinking. Constant attendance collided with my responsibilities of school and other secular demands. Once I graduated from UNF, I had a great deal more time to spend on rehashing all the notebooks I collected in which I filled with notes from first principal classes. That training was, without a doubt, my awakening and deliverance from the digression into movements.

It is character changes or sanctification that God is interested in once one is saved, not the constant pleading for outward manifestations, for God's place is in the heart, in the inner man. Our visible bodies are merely containers that allow us to decrease while the Lord increases.

The Holy Spirit, then, is less of a power player, than a revealer of Biblical truths. He gives enlightenment to the Scriptures and adds understanding to students concerning the passages they read. The Holy Spirit is quickened upon initial salvation to give a Christian the ability to grasp the Scriptures.

I understand many believers in this day desire to see the outworking of whatever it is the Holy Spirit is said to possess as listed in 1st Cor 12. Those gifts or operations are listed as a word of wisdom, a word of knowledge, faith, gifts of healing, the working of miracles, prophecy, the discerning of spirits, tongues, and the interpretation of tongues.

And so, some churches prefer to major more on attempts to produce the manifestation of all these gifts in operation, and think they are the major intent of the Christian life, which leaves out the very important necessity for the Word of God to be studied, meditated upon, preached, taught, and memorized. So wrong it is for God's Word to be the missing part in most of the Charismatic or continuationist gatherings today that believe in the gifts as never having parted from the church. Their misguided bent has caused them to dismiss the building of sound doctrine.

The notion of sanctification through a daily process of giving oneself to the Word of God, to prayer, and to some type of personal giving, is a lost approach among Charismatics, as their intent is nothing more than to experience a kind of emotional state that is anticipated at the end of their gatherings, especially those where the membership runs in the thousands. Leadership's maneuvering is set by their use of live music, which, in ways, tends to express a more carnal sensation than one that should draw one into the presence of God. In many of the fringe Charismatic groups these days, there is the use of black lights and glowing attire as well as the more sensual musical undergirding that secular concerts create.

Very few Charismatics have strong foundations in the first principles listed in Hebrews 6 because they know nothing of them. Instead, they seek to feel emotional rushes, to fall, to witness miracles, to dance or jump around, to even fall all over one another in a display that supposedly proves the existence of God's presence during their gathering.

CHAPTER 23:

John Piper

The pastor who best describes this phenomenon is John Piper, a Reformist Charismatic. I've taken word-for-word from one of his talks. It is excellent instruction.

"There are many doctrinal abuses in the Charismatic church where experience is elevated above doctrine and doctrine is made minimally important. It's a huge defect in many Charismatic churches. The fear is, if you try to study the Bible with a view to assembling a coherent view of doctrine, you are going to quench the spirit and you will not have as much vitality in your heart because the mind and the heart are at odds with each other. That's a mistake, an abuse of experience to make it the enemy or the alternative to doctrine.

"The Bible is sometimes used as an instrument in the priming of the pump of phenomena. What the attendees really want in the room is some fireworks. They want someone to fall, or someone to laugh, or someone to tremble, or somebody to raise their hands, or someone to hear a word of extraordinary prophecy such as, "there's a man in a red shirt in the audience, he's going to Argentina next week," and nobody can know that except the prophet.

"You want all that stuff to happen, then what do you do with the Bible? You use it like pouring water into a pump, and everybody knows, you don't care anything about this text, you don't care anything about this sermon. You are using this sermon to get us ready for the fireworks in the end which we used to call ministry time."

After I moved to Tampa, and after trying as seriously as I could to find a church to call home, I was even more bewildered by the lack of any group whose primary emphasis with young believers is anything but to get them well established in the Word of God. For many years now, I have set aside belonging, when, in the past, I felt it was so important to fit into a group. Groups today are full of various divergences regarding every aspect of the Christian life, so I've chosen to remain at home, stick to my daily Bible studies kept for years in my stacks of notebooks from the first principal teachings, to pray, and to only occasionally meet with a group.

It's been the right choice. After noticing what evolved once mega-churches began to be the norm, I knew the Word was destined to be laid aside. Just as John Piper wrote, those mega-groups have grown obsessively emotion ridden with so little Word coming from behind the pulpit, that I was grateful I had my long-held notebooks to keep me from starving for the truth, as opposed to what I perceived to be made-up sermons formed from God's whispering in the ears of the leading men in charge, all in response to needing justification for having steered the basically unlearned Charismatic church into another wild extreme.

Through my study of the Scriptures, I found myself very recognizably being divorced, separated, and delivered from the strong, misguided mystical side of the Charismatic masses. To my stunning amazement, that move brought me strength, not weakness. I no longer felt the need to run off to one misconceived and erroneous playground after another. By opening my Bible on a consistent basis, rehashing those first principles with as much attention as is needed to understand a particular point, I stay well able to discern what

I hear from one YouTube preacher after another. I ask, is this true? Does it line up with the Word of God or not?

What I discovered is that there are absolutely no emotion-centered and emotion-driven gatherings to be found in the Scriptures. In the days of the First Church, I could see there was no proof that the intent of all their gatherings was to wait on what Piper calls the "fireworks." And so, I have opted to remain very cautious, to take a back seat to movements in general. For, as I see them, they are centuries ahead in emotionalism, and are run more like the very understudied playgrounds of the old Pentecostal meetings from the 1910s.

Did I ever go running around, dancing, and displaying foolishness, thinking it was actually some sort of blessing from the Holy Ghost? Sure, I did, and I probably danced more than most in my earliest days in the Lord. But what has evolved today is nothing like that at all. Instead, there is an entire hierarchy saturated by a conspiracy intent on getting every dime from the pockets of those who attend or are given to following the misled. All it takes is to tickle the ears of the youth. Get them dancing and feeling party hardy.

In the early days following my divorce I tried a Four-Square Church in Tampa, whose pastor said we were all to go outside, hold hands as we stood around the church, and rebuke the devil for having stolen all of the church's PA equipment which had gone missing over the past two days. We would get back those electronics, he told us, because God showed him that was to be the case. His actions were nothing more than youthful Pentecostalism.

Next time, sitting in the church, I realized I was not where I needed to be, so I got out of my seat and walked to my car, never to return. Churches after that one were no different, as most were in infantile stages of the Spirit-filled life and enormously emotion-driven; in other words, they were filled with traps, and not one of them was actually Word-oriented, but rather WOF centered.

"Believe me when I tell you, if you want deliverance in your life, and I mean real deliverance, you must know what it is that is the cause of your disillusionment. Without seeking out the cause, you will remain in a grip that is extremely hard to find a release.

"The Word is insignificant to those who use it for nothing more than a springboard for their spiritual calisthenics, where they boost their feelings to the point of displaying some form of an outward sign of God's manifest presence. I personally sense that there would be no need to fill church offices if the Word was dwelling richly in the souls of saints, if they permitted those passages to dwell richly in each believer rather than the focus being on this one man or woman who has taken the lead over everything from the messages being delivered to the control of the purse strings of the assembly.

Solomon wrote, "Labour not to be rich." (Prov. 23:4) We can expect the Lord to bless and prosper us, to provide an income for our families or to those to whom we feel responsible, but our devoted attention should not be for wealth and fame. For, just to be rich, famous, and have a great reputation is much less than what the Lord desires for us. His principal desire is that we permit Him to inwardly change us, to make us humble and selfless, to help us to lay aside every weight of sin, to run the race, to mortify the deeds of the flesh, to put on Christ, and all those wonderful metaphors that speak of our sanctification or the deliverance from the power of sin in our lives.

CHAPTER 24:

Active Listening

A brother in the Lord, Skip Hunt, I met at a home fellowship. After the service, he and I talked about his work in what was being labeled a tele-ministry by those familiar with this Christian counseling approach. Already, I'd spent a couple of years volunteering time for another such group known as Lovelines, but Skip offered training that sounded enormously beneficial. Rather than experiment with how to reply to distressed callers, Skip held classes he called *How Can I Help?*, which was also the title of his manual. It taught the counselor to respond to the caller with words that encouraged him/her to open up, eventually leading to a solution. Once the prevailing emotions were identified, the situation changed ownership from blaming the offender to dealing with the caller's feelings.

It is a fairly simple method yet used so little in everyday conversation with others. Instead of owning what is being expressed directly to you, one must learn to allow the potential offender to own what he/she expressed. This is done by mirroring the speaker's words either by paraphrasing them or phrasing their words exactly. An example would be if someone spoke to me in a harsh tone, or any tone for that matter, or passed judgment, or made a statement that was meant to embarrass or ridicule me. My reply, I learned, was to be: "You really don't like me, do you?" or "I've upset you, haven't I?"

When talking on the phone, that same approach is used to counsel hurting individuals. Its intent is to focus on the person's emotions in a way that lets them hear themselves and shows them that they own their own emotions, not the person to whom they have addressed.

When on the phone, a caller might say, "My husband will not treat me well at all. I clean the house, cook for him, and I'm always doing errands for him, yet he seems not to notice that I exist." I might reply by mirroring her statement with, "Wow, you feel your husband does not notice all that you do for him. That makes you upset." In reply, I might hear, "You're damn right, he hates me; I can feel it." My reply could be merely paraphrased by stating her emotions. "You're really upset."

This counseling approach is designed to help release all that the hurting caller is feeling. Eventually, the counselor will lead the conversation into identifying the feelings. He might suggest the identity of feelings, but it is best when the caller realizes them on his or her own. Then the counselor will ask the caller, "What have you tried to do to alleviate this problem?" They might list a few things, such as: "I thought if I asked his father to address his son that he's ignoring me, he might shake him out of it, but he doesn't want to get involved," or "I talked to my pastor, and he prayed for me. What else am I to do?"

So many children, as well as adults, are desperately in need of a listening ear, someone who can help them hear themselves, which will lead them to better understand what it is they are wrestling with. I was never once approached by a single adult, whether related or otherwise, who approached me to discuss the aftermath of my mother's attempted suicide.

How was I feeling? What thoughts did I have? Was I thinking clearly? Was I depressed?

A strong fallacy in those days was the thought that all children are resilient; they always bounce back no matter their challenges. Children were thought to be capable of healing from an emotional experience no matter the intensity. Don't believe it! Nothing could be further from the truth.

The condition that my siblings and I developed following our mother's first attempt is called Post Traumatic Stress Disorder or PTSD, but in the early sixties, there was no name for it. Neither was it recognized. Children were left alone with their thoughts and feelings, left to struggle through the inner turmoil without a guide or hope. Listening to a child who's been under duress is so important! But it wasn't to be in my family. Instead, we carried out into our worlds, into the military, academia, and the church, the blocked, unexpressed hurts and feelings that even the promises of a prayer life seldom alleviated.

Kids invariably hear the same thoughts in their heads, repeated over and over, year after year, while trying to make sense of a senseless emotional event that clings to them during the preceding phases of their lives.

For many decades, where I grew up, thirty miles north of Pittsburgh, few fathers could display affection. The most prevalent emotions they held were distrust, negativity, fatalism, and bigotry. Fathers, within the general community, during my boyhood, were inappropriately distant and uninvolved with their children. Targets for their criticism existed everywhere, including government bodies, the school system, the workplace, nationalities, and strangers. Taking the brunt of their lack of friendliness were their kids who were invisible, ignored, discounted, and/or criticized.

Without psych tools such as Active Listening, as well as the conviction of the existence of solid absolute truths and the ability to convey those life-giving words, kids, too, will remain, essentially, alone.

Boys would be gone from the house for most of the day without parental concern, and when attempts were made to consult their fathers about the challenges of growing up, they were told to toughen up, be a man and not cry. If the child refused or had difficulty adopting that hardened facade, he was considered weak.

Every household contained plant workers and non-academic union workers, many of whom barely graduated high school. Most of them were in possession of a strong work ethic as well as an equally strong drinking habit. Found inside many of the fraternal organizations was a thriving camaraderie. Every day, after work, they sat around the bar bullshitting about the latest injustices.

My father never attended the first concert in which I played nor a minor league baseball game in which I pitched. Overall, fathers understood little of the much-needed affectionate mental health care their wives and children craved. The millwork culture exuded little warmth or genuine caring, for sarcasm was the leading response to most everything in life. Emotional needs were not to be discussed, and if one attempted to seek consolement, the words were either ignored, the child scolded, or reform school was threatened.

Talks with so-called psychiatric professionals were either frowned upon or entirely nonexistent because the patient would be labeled by their peers as insane. If a family member was sent to a psychiatrist, it was to be kept hushed from others. There were no chemical treatments in those days. Instead, psychiatrists would often resort to primitive means like lobotomies and shock treatments.

Then, as if a Renaissance arrived, one-on-one counseling was entirely set aside, seldomly employed. Pills became the treatment of choice by the system. Often, a mental health problem within the home was ignored by parents in the 60s for fear of airing one's dirty laundry. And so, the afflicted, without a listening ear, grew worse, which time and again could potentially lead to suicide.

"We'll take care of our own problems. We don't need anyone interfering in our business. Leave us alone. We'll take care of our own" were the words often heard when anyone outside the family, say, a school counselor, suspected trouble brewing at home or in the mind of the student.

All sorts of brain abnormalities were left to run rampant, from deep depression, schizophrenia, bipolar, and OCD, to just plain weirdness. Even fellow students could see the inner turmoil of an odd student, whom they labeled with terms like mentally retarded, retardo, retard, or having a screw loose.

CHAPTER 25:

My Start at FJC

Three months after my naval discharge, knowing I had the GI Bill to help with providing me an education, I enrolled in the local FJC (Florida Junior College). Not in possession of a vehicle, as my van had long since died, I hitched rides to the campus and worked various jobs to help with tuition costs. I chose to major in music and, with the money I saved one dime at a time, I purchased an upright bass which I played in a symphonic band.

It was 1973, a usual day of walking and thumbing in the central Florida tropical sun. I was nineteen years old and in my first year of attendance at the junior college where I intended to earn an AA in music. Slung around my shoulder was the loop attached to the leather sleeve into which I inserted my double bass bow. The leather case was made by friends whose leather shop was located below the first-story apartment I shared with another brother in Christ, Bruce. The leather shop owner was Dan Pauly, and Richard Bailey was his one employee. Both were Christians and a part of the Jesus Movement of the early 70s in Jacksonville Beach. They made an assortment of the most stunning leather goods and were great friends to have when I needed a good laugh.

Two backpacks I carried, one to tote my books and papers, and the other into which I placed the empty soda bottles I found lying on the roadside as

I hitched rides to and from the college campus. Their deposit value would afford me my one meal of the day which I would eat after classes in the cafeteria located at the rear of a large grocery store called Pic N Save. The price was a mere two dollars. That food kept me alive, not putting any real weight on my bones but it produced energy enough to continue the same hitching of rides.

I never weighed much throughout my boyhood and teenage years. At five-foot-ten and 121 pounds, I enlisted in the Navy. How fortunate I was to grow to 132 pounds through boot camp, after eating three meals each day. My poor life as a college student quickly caused me to lose those few extra pounds. So embarrassed I was of my thinness, I would always wear socks to hide my especially thin calves. And I never wore shorts to the campus, even while I hitchhiked to and from classes in scorching weather. It was blue jeans I wore, and how I wished it to be otherwise.

Florida's spring and summer sun can be brutal. It certainly had its way with my skin. I don't believe I was ever as dark-tanned as I was in those days. Friends tell me today that my neck and arms are a startling difference in color. At 70, I'm a far distance from being that twenty-three-year-old dedicated student who fried as he hitched rides. To add to my color was the fact that it took me seven years to complete a four-year degree.

One day, while thumbing alongside the highway, a 60s VW van stopped to offer me a ride. "Where are you headed, buddy?" I was asked.

"To the Jr. College. It's up ahead on the right."

"Oh yeah, I stop there every day when I get to my class. I teach religion at the college. You like religion?" he asked.

He was an especially handsome man. I knew the girls would go nuts over him. Plus, he was soft-spoken and had a gentle kindness. His dark, medium-cut hair proved he wasn't entirely without a bit of post-hippie influence and his easy manner indicated he believed–but what?

"Do I like religion? My whole life is nothing but an immersion into the Jesus Movement, which I doubt I will ever lay aside. It's a little more than a fad. The local anti-establishment, hippie-like, sandal-wearing, long hairs (my often-used description, in those days, of Christian friends) meet in homes and talk about Bible beliefs they pick up from books, tapes and radio sermons of their favorite Charismatic preachers. They talk, for instance, of guidelines to stick to that will keep a believer from losing his salvation. One of the first things I noticed was that they're very anti-denominational and extremely suspicious of anyone who supports seminary training. Seminaries to them are cemeteries, where the dead go. Those places, they say, aren't life giving. They enjoy their independence from denominations who frown on speaking in tongues and miracles.

"All the Christians I know are young, and already they talk about what ministry they feel God is leading them into, even though they are short of preparation, unless they see themselves as becoming an evangelist because it's those verses, we first learned, like John 3:16. They share tapes of sermons made by faith pushers mostly.

"Some of the guys are asking God to direct them to their wives, and already a few of them have told girls that God showed them they are to be married. It's a culture that continues to grow on its own, inside and outside of itself. It appears like we're adopting someone's way of life we don't see."

"You have a calling, do you?" he asked, smiling enigmatically.

"I suppose so, at least that's what I'm being told, that God places every one of His sons and daughters into places where their particular gifts are of some use."

"What gifts do you have? Oh, by the way, my name is Patrick." He held his hand out.

"I'm Dave." I offered mine, and he gave it a friendly shake.

"Why don't you enroll in my class? I'll bet. With all the connections you have within the school there's sure to be other Christian friends who would be willing to join you. Assignments won't be difficult because anything a person believes is what they believe. How can I dispute their conclusions? But then, maybe I can help them to broaden their perspectives, you think?"

"They're a hard-nosed bunch, Charismatics, and can't be talked out of their views, that is, if they have actually formulated anything beyond the Charismatic experience. What is it that religion professors call them—continuationists? We all are that to the hilt. But I can't speak for all of them because most have barely dug themselves into the study of their Bibles other than to memorize a few verses on faith and the Holy Ghost baptism."

"I plan to look at things in less of a dogmatic fashion and examine Christianity as the progression of events brought on by various criteria. What was promised in the Old Testament, for instance, was said to be fulfilled in the New. Do you see that?"

"Do I believe all prophecies have been fulfilled?"

"Have they? What are they, do you know?"

"I don't know many of them. The easiest, of course, is Isaiah 53 as the precursor to the life of Jesus and the giveaway chapter for His sacrifice. But I don't see much more than simple examples."

"That's simple? Isaiah 53 must be the most controversial of all Jewish texts, even to this day. Many Jewish priests pass over that chapter because it so well represents the life of Christ. They don't want that chapter to cause doubt in the minds of their fellow Jews.

"Maybe that's a topic you could choose to write on. What scares the Jewish reader from giving Isaiah a close look? Do you know of any Jews who open their texts to look at what was written prophetically?"

I shook my head thoughtfully. "I don't know any Jews, not a one."

He grinned. "Well then, maybe this is the time. Visit a synagogue, go to where Jews might hang out, and kindly discuss what they believe. That would make a great paper," he said, adding in a comic tone, "Around this corner is my parking space unless that sexy art teacher took it again. I don't mind when that happens. She's a real looker."

The spot we took wasn't far from the second-floor doorway, so we walked in together. He mentioned he was seriously considering enrolling at Florida State University in Tallahassee to work on his Ph.D. He asked if I thought his house could be useful to a few young, responsible men who would keep it in good condition while he and his family sojourned for a year.

"That sounds great to me, Pat; I'll ask a few brothers I know."

Living on 1st Avenue North, in Jacksonville Beach, with another brother, Bruce, with whom I shared a landscape business, the timing for a move seemed perfect. We had three months to pack, as that was when Pat was planning his move to Tallahassee.

I called numerous friends to ask if they wanted to join Bruce and me and discovered two brothers delighted to come along, Rick and Billy. The house's pool was an added incentive.

"There's a good-sized garage at this new place, Billy, so if you want to do some side work, it would be perfect for it, just as long as you kept the floor as clean as you found it," I said.

"Sounds good to me," he replied. His country accent put me much at home, having spent years among hard-working Appalachian mechanics, and he liked to laugh, which relaxed anyone who was around him. He found humor in everything.

Rick liked the idea of moving to a more centralized area. Driving the town from one activity to another made his life. He didn't need a job as he was well set up after a bundle fell on his lap a few years prior and left him without worry. He took me to free costume parades and plays whose refreshments I could barely afford. Our time away was always enjoyable and gave me a break from the books.

Pat's place was ideal for all of us. We were all thinking good thoughts about making the change of address, but first, we agreed to pray about it.

Standing in a circle, Bruce led the prayer, "Lord Jesus, You know best Your will for us. We ask You to confirm to us if we should move. Everything looks good. Is it in your will, and if it is, would you please make it go easy and give us the dedication to keep Patrick's house in excellent shape? We offer You praise and thanksgiving for being our ever-present help. In Jesus' name, Amen."

Bruce wanted badly to get away from the small apartment we shared as he longed for more adequate parking, to allow for his car and the trailer which carried our lawn care equipment. We had a small, prospering gardening business, which helped to earn enough money to purchase better gear. Also, the income helped me to purchase a 1971 VW Bug. I bought it from an old friend from where I used to live on Azalea Place. What a joy it was to have my own transportation. I was through with hitchhiking.

I'd only owned that bug a few months when I was shocked to discover it "stolen" from my parking spot just below the staircase leading to the ground floor of our boardwalk apartment. Immediately, I rushed to the police station, which was a mere three blocks from the lot, where I gave the police a photo of my car. I'd labeled the back window in large letters, "Jesus is God", and I wondered why anyone would want to steal something so noticeable.

It turned out the police had intentionally impounded my car for reasons I was never given. Then, they lied, saying they found my vehicle in the city of Jacksonville with a bum inside driving it. I eventually discovered they had towed it from my parking spot, thinking a tourist had wrongly parked in my small space. My Bug was in good condition, not at all junkyard scrap. From my appointed parking space, my car was impounded, and the police kept lying to me through the entire ordeal.

"Don't worry about anything," a policeman said, "the man is under arrest. We'll take care of the rest. It's just good to see you have your car back." Every word of that statement was a lie. It was indeed a relief to have my Bug returned to me, but the police refused to turn over my vehicle until I paid towing costs. I was a college student on a very limited budget and had to borrow from the Beaches Chapel bookkeeper, Jim Messinese, the required fifty dollars to get my car returned to me when I did nothing to earn such a penalty. I stopped trusting the police department from that day forward. But that wouldn't be the last time they interfered with my life.

CHAPTER 26:

Semester Break – Episode 1

O ne spring day, while living on First Street in Jacksonville Beach, Florida, my brother Denny and I were walking the back stairs of the complex, not knowing what activities were to fill the day. We took our seats in my VW Bug; I backed up, and off we went.

I asked Denny, "You want to get something to eat?"

"No, not much money, just a few bucks in the bank."

"I'll just drive then. We'll figure something out. How about we head for the jetties to watch them fish?"

"Nah, nothing going on there."

I drove in a western direction.

This is hard to believe but very much the truth. In four days, we pulled into the parking lot of the San Diego, California YMCA.

We had debated what to do. Getting away was important for both of us. Hitting I-10 going west, we didn't stop until we got tired. At 567 miles beyond the beach, we drove into downtown New Orleans, onto Bourbon Street, pulled over where a gathering of vagabonds huddled and discovered we'd stumbled onto the city's soup kitchen and sleeping quarters. They fed us the most horrendous cold rice and beans and sent us into a room where we sat to listen to the gospel being preached, after which we waited for the "all clear" to hit our racks.

In the morning, we grabbed a piece of rotted fruit and headed outside to the car. Once on the road, we stopped at the home of one of the Christian brothers who also got his Bible training in the six principle foundational teachings, except he was taught by Doug Westmoreland, the initial adopter of the Bible lessons originated by the Six Principle Baptists which he adopted, then added Charismatic truths to the syllabus. Reb lived in Beaumont, Texas at the time he sat under Doug's training. He now lived in Shreveport, a 314-mile drive from The Big Easy. I will never forget his kindness.

In the evenings, we sat outside and talked on topics regarding the state of the church and cited most of the church's refusal to receive solid, first principal teachings. I don't recall what dessert his wife prepared for us, but unlike our normal fast-food fare, I remember the taste was superb.

Somehow, I lost the key to my Bug, so without a key, it had to be pushed to pop the clutch. We continued to pop it any time we stopped, from California, back to Jacksonville Beach. It lacked a working solenoid. I did eventually get one once we returned home.

The next night, we slept in a Baptist mission on the church floor, located northeast of Shreveport, in Colorado. Nothing much happened there. We walked in, were provided blankets, selected a pew, fell asleep, and again awoke to rotting fruit offered as breakfast. We ate prunes this time.

We passed through a vast length of uninhabited canyons and buttes painted in varied brown colors. Not a soul seemed to live among those vast, gorgeous plateaus except buffalo. Barren territories of unmatched beauty blanketed the land.

Rocky mountain browns made up of thousands of shades impressed me. Seeing those lands made it easy for me to understand how possessive various Indian tribes were, and still are. The territory existed as a spiritual place for them, and indeed, it felt transcendent.

Along the highway were rest stops where travelers could pull over to take a break. They weren't as well-furnished as those on the best roads, but then, I grew tired of looking, so I pulled over, got out of the car, grabbed a sleeping bag that Reb gave me, walked to a table in a vacant lot at a very early morning hour, and dozed off on a tabletop.

A couple of hours later, after a dream formed, a highway patrol officer awakened me.

He shook my shoulder and asked, "What are you doing? Why are you here? You're sleeping under my stars. I don't appreciate it when I catch people sleeping under my stars. You're under my stars. I don't want that." He reminded me of the bigoted Carol O'Connor role in *The Heat of the Night*.

"I'm tired, and because my VW doesn't have a lot of room, I rested here. My brother is in the car. It doesn't bother him that much because I do most of the driving and have that steering wheel. Can't I get at least another couple of hours of sleep?"

"No, I want you off this table so you can open your car for me. I'm going to inspect it."

"For what? I own nothing illegal."

"That's what they say," he said. "Open it. You resemble hippies to me. Are you a couple of hippies? We don't allow hippies in this state. Now, get over here and open this."

So, I did, which required only the push of a button on the front hood to look inside for contraband. A quick glance into the interior, and he was done. Both my glove compartment and my trunk held nothing more than hundreds of Chick tracts that I used to witness to strangers.

"I use those to share the gospel of Christ. I'm a Christian who enjoys sharing his faith and the testimony of what Jesus Christ has done for me, both through His forgiveness of my sins and for strengthening me in my weaknesses."

"You're going to experience a terrible weakness if you stay here another minute," he said. "I want you on your way this second. Pack whatever you might have outside your car and drive away."

"As you can see, I am only an avid evangelist. I enjoy sharing the gospel. Have you heard of it? Do you know what Jesus did for you? I'll be happy to share the truth of the gospel with you. He can change your life."

"No, I have no time for such silliness. It's a complete waste, a stupid story someone created to make money. Nobody can prove the first part of it. Fakers made it up to bamboozle the vulnerable. Now, go on, get in your car, and get out of here."

So, back on the road I drove, after popping the clutch and putting it in gear.

I drove toward Salt Lake City with my sights on reaching Reno, Nevada, located five hundred miles away on a more northwestern route to California. Once past San Francisco, the highway kept us viewing the California coastline, which, after 501 miles, would lead us into San Diego. I remember driving past the Hearst mansion. A bridge ran high above the sandy beach where I pulled over and parked. I wanted to take in the scenery. The Pacific Ocean view is so much different than the Atlantic Ocean. There are rocks, steep hills, larger waves, and a surface that seems higher, creating a magnetic environment.

In San Diego, we planned to reunite with George. He'd left behind a head shop on Jacksonville Beach and returned to his hometown. But he remained unable to visit with us, and so we sought sleeping accommodations.

A surprise awaited us as I drove to the San Diego YMCA. Just as I pulled up, a guy came walking down the front steps. He stopped to ask me if we needed a room.

"I have another two days here. This is my key. Take it; take a long hot shower. Then relax. You'll be glad you did." Indeed, an angel rescued us.

Opening the door, we discovered two full-sized beds.

We had to be the happiest two people on earth. We parked the Bug and ran up to our room. How inviting the bed looked. They served simple meals at the YMCA, so we accepted the handouts and fell back to sleep, repeatedly awakening, then snoring. We accomplished little while in that city. Sleep, shower, then sleep some more.

After two nights passed, I suggested we get underway, only this time it was to drive east toward Florida. We asked a few guys to help us push the Bug to pop the clutch, and began making headway, east on the 8, to the 10.

We stocked the car with corn chips and beer and could not fathom the utter lack of familiarity once we hit that large, bright, dry oven. The gas in the car read low, so I pulled into a gas station that claimed to be the last one before the desert ended.

"How do you live out here in this heat and barrenness?" I asked the young proprietor.

"Oh, it's nothing. All my life, born and raised in this desert. I tried getting away twice but kept coming back. Now that my parents are dead, I run the place and enjoy it this way. There's no one to bother me. I'm happy."

"Did you ever consider enlistment in the military?"

"They won't take me. I have too many health issues for them to accept me, and besides, I'm content here."

"You married?"

"No, it's just me and my dog, Brownie. Here Brownie, come here, boy." He looked around for him to introduce me, but Brownie must have been asleep on the other side of the building.

"Don't you miss things? What about movie theaters or restaurants?"

"Oh, I sometimes will close the station to take a drive to the cities, but in no time, I miss the quiet of my home and leave. I have a TV that picks up a few stations. All one needs is the news so as not to exist in the dark. I figure it's important to know what's going on in the world."

"Now that we're here, do you have the need for a hand, a job that is too hard for you to do by yourself? You've got four extra hands here. We can help you before we leave."

"I do have this enormous tire a trucker left me. I can't get it positioned right. Would you be willing….?"

"Sure, don't worry, we'll have it moved where you want." We got it pulled away from an enormous pile of odds-and-ends, then rolled it to the side of the storage shed to keep it out of the heat.

He offered us each a Nehi crush, which we drank in seconds.

"We'd better get going. What's your name? Gee, we never got around to that, did we?" I asked.

"Fred Nealy," he said, "and yours?" We explained our likeness in appearance, and Fred said he imagined it from the moment we met.

"I am a bit more handsome. That's where the confusion comes in," I said. Fred laughed. We said our goodbyes.

The Bug got farther and farther from Fred's gas station as we drove west. I'll never forget that trip.

CHAPTER 27:

Semester Break–Episode 2

I was to learn the hard way just how unlikable I must have appeared with my long hair and beard–the only reason I could imagine was that a group of short-haired, holier-than-thou cops had reason to badger me.

While on semester break during my college days, I was midway through the reading of Alexandre I. Solzhenitsyn's personal account of Stalin's terror-filled reign, *Gulag Archipelago*. It is not an easy read, especially for those who prefer to not acquaint themselves with the harshest realities of life.

Knowing something about terror and the madness of dysfunction as a boy, in an odd way I looked forward to finding equal treatment in those pages. Instead of that, however, I discovered profound courage and spiritual strength. I was in awe of the Russian people and sympathetic toward their horrific ordeal.

Then, while in the middle of the book, I got a knock on my apartment door. I arose, opened it, and was met face-to-face with a man identifying himself as an agent while holding FBI credentials. Accompanying him were another FBI agent and a police officer.

The guy at first seemed to be in charge. He and his men, he told me, had been keeping my apartment under surveillance for the past few days and wondered why I chose not to leave, why I remained cooped up. "Are you hiding? You haven't left that seat (pointing) for hours, and you've been out only once to order food at Benny's," he said.

My completely honest explanation to the FBI was that I was a poor college student who was attempting to get a head start on reading assignments for the next term. "I'm majoring in literature, and the workload can be overwhelming at times," I said.

Benny's Chinese restaurant was my favorite place to eat. Located only a few minutes from the beach shoreline, my apartment was across the street from the best Chinese food I will likely eat in my life, on the second story, above a leather shop, directly across from Benny's.

To get there, I had to leave the building down the back stairwell behind Dan's leather shop. The smell of fresh cut leather and dyes I grew to like, and often I stepped in to chat for a while, mostly about Christian life issues. I had fun with Rich's many sarcastic critiques of the most often mentioned doctrinal topics that were shaping the paths of hundreds of misled, dedicated listeners.

Richard, Dan's helper, was a phenomenal craftsman and entertained us with his impersonations. It was all so intense, those years we shared, every day wrapped up in a community-wide movement that demanded inward and outward change. One had to laugh to exist in a culture that so ravaged all we once thought normal.

Both Richard and I were musicians in an original Christian trio that placed Richard as the lead singer, and rightfully so. A crowd-pleaser, he could have everyone in stitches any time he spoke. The laughs were medicinal and sought by disheartened and discouraged believers who realized living out the Christian life was the hardest thing in this life to do.

So, back to the authorities at my door. "What's this all about?" I asked him. His reply was as if it jumped right out of the pages I was reading, "You fit the composite of a man who raped and murdered a girl thirty miles south of here. We're taking you in for questioning."

To them, I must not have displayed any worry or guilt because they didn't handcuff me. "Surely, there's been some mistake," I told myself.

The police station was located less than three blocks from my apartment, and during our slow walk there, the agent asked me what else I did with my leisure time. I told him that I liked to fish.

"What kind of fish do you catch?" Their questions, I later realized, were intended to discern whether I was truly an angler.

"Whiting and flounder mostly," I replied.

"Where do you go?" he asked in a further attempt to catch me.

"Mostly to the pier, but flounder are best caught at night near the jetties in Mayport," I replied as we entered the station.

Past the doorway, I was told to take a seat inside a scarcely furnished foyer. The agent continued his disguise. He told me he and his buddy planned to do some fishing while they were in Florida and asked if I had any pointers to share with them. I explained how to set fishing lines and the type of bait to use.

"Have I passed the test?" I thought to ask, but I just let it go.

After ten minutes, I was led into a room where my fingerprints were taken, thanked for being cooperative, and told not to leave town for a few weeks. I complied.

Never again was I called to the police station, and I never learned if they caught the bad guy.

When I got back to my apartment, I picked up Solzhenitsyn's book and read: "It was granted me to carry away from my prison years on my bent back, which nearly broke beneath its load, this essential experience; how a human being becomes evil and how good....And it was only when I lay there on rotting prison straw that I sensed within myself the first stirrings of good.

"Gradually it was disclosed to me that the line separating good and evil passes not through states, nor between classes, nor between political parties either—but right through every human heart—and through all human hearts. This line shifts. Inside us, it oscillates with the years. And even within hearts overwhelmed by evil, one small bridgehead of good is retained. And even in the best of all hearts, there remains… an unuprooted small corner of evil. ``

I never did see those guys at the jetties.

I needed the money to continue my schooling at UNF, and so, after a couple of years of mowing lawns, laying sod, and creating plant beds, I sold my portion of the business to Bruce for $500, which was enough for me to return to classes while I searched for a part-time job. Lucky for me, the campus was having its student body elections, so I submitted my name as a candidate for the position of Student Government Secretary. The outcome was a tie with the counted votes against another male student. There was enough work for the two of us, so the President treated us equally by making secretaries of us both.

Eventually, after too many years had passed attending the Jr. College, I was still without a graduation date. Far too many one-credit courses made up the curriculum, so I transferred all my credits to a general associate degree, enabling me to graduate.

Days later, I enrolled at the University of North Florida to acquire a more academic major–English/Literature. I graduated in 1980 owing only $1,200. Because I owed, no matter the amount, it kept me from being awarded my sheepskin. Then, in 1989, I chose to enter grad school, and I sent for my transcripts at UNF. Within the return correspondence, I was informed my debt was forgiven. That allowed me to enter USF to work on a master's in public administration.

CHAPTER 28:

Austin to Ohio

A t the end of my naval enlistment, I moved around for various reasons.
The last place I lived in Jacksonville Beach was a rental apartment with a
female Christian singer named Teri whose voice was captivating. It was while
talking with her one afternoon that I realized there might be a place for me
in Austin, Texas with my twin brother, Denny. We both played guitars, and
putting together a band, I felt, was something we might easily do.

The drive to Austin held little more than the tediousness of the road. I'd
spent so much time in cars as a boy, I thought, what was another fifteen hours
and over a thousand miles? On the drive, I could imagine nothing more than
the fact that Denny was awaiting my arrival. I thought, once settled in, we
could arrive at a common purpose, but it wasn't to be.

Instead, I spent my days seeking a job and/or writing. At one point,
I realized I needed the use of reference materials. Computers had not yet
come on the scene, so I drove to the University of Texas library, browsed the
shelves, and selected a few books that appeared helpful, but the checkout
clerk told me it was not allowed. I either had to be a student of the university
or pay for an annual library card at the price of $45, a lot more than I had in
my pockets being unemployed. Undaunted, I drove back to the apartment

complex, found a shady place under a tree, and wrote an article that a week later I sold to a Christian magazine for a whopping fifteen dollars.

Once reunited, I felt some happiness in seeing Denny. For income, he and his wife, Sherelle, managed an apartment complex full of illegal Mexican border crossers. As many as a dozen of them would fill an apartment, and if they grew to be a nuisance, Sherelle would boot them out. She'd tell them that disgruntled tenants called the police and that they were on their way to inspect the premises. The news caught the Mexicans totally unprepared and unsuspecting, and forced them to flee with the barest necessities, leaving behind furniture which Denny and Sherelle sold to either store proprietors or piece by piece to others in the complex.

My visit to Austin would be short-lived as Denny's partner judged me to be in the way–a magnet of a sort that would draw my brother away from her. She needed him to care for the upkeep of the complex and to have herself a drinking buddy. Still, I hung out as long as possible, hoping I could find other accommodations. Without a doubt, I needed a job, which became a definite challenge.

When not calling businesses, most of which were labor-oriented, my writing earned me a few dollars scribbling short articles for Christian magazines. I had to find a real forty-hour-a-week position fast, either writing for some publication or laboring on a construction site.

Finally, time ran out. Denny's wife insisted I leave. She feared that if I stayed any longer, I'd eventually persuade Denny to abandon her, a redhead who lived on Black Velvet, liked TV soap operas, kept a clean house, disliked fancy attire, and cared little for money apart from what would meet her addiction needs. Her lifestyle was entirely different from mine in so many ways. I didn't drink, nor did I smoke weed. I wasn't much of a candidate for whatever partying others asked me to join in.

I'd made a friend. He was an oil rigger who flew by helicopter into the Gulf and was dropped off onto various rigs that needed him. It's funny to me still that this fellow greatly enjoyed composing smut novels in his spare time. After discussing our writing, Bob tried to persuade me to give porn a shot. It was so funny to me to think of writing such stuff. I almost gave in to doing it if it hadn't been for the fact, I knew I would have to explain the love process in so many varied forms, with similes and metaphors that filled volumes, so I chose not to join him.

Bob used to recite a long list of metaphors he had memorized after a couple of years of writing smut. Truth is, I was impressed by what it took to write different love-making scenes. The idea kept me amused, even though I asked myself, "Shouldn't you react in a more condemning fashion?" The humor refused to fade.

One night, when Denny's wife, Sherelle, was drunk and raving mad, Denny and I loaded my car and drove north, desiring to check out Chicago. I suggested we join up with the Jesus People USA Christian community in Chicago. A band formed there in 1972, known as the Resurrection Band or Rez Band or REZ. It was not exactly our genre of Christian music, but it encouraged me to pursue joining someone with a good voice with whom we could play his/her tracks. Those believers in Chicago understood evangelism was important, a direction opposed to what I was seeing in Florida. Those on the beach leaned strongly to the obsessive showing up for meeting after meeting, warming one folding chair after another, merely to listen to another sermon with the same prosperity message spoken by those who plagiarized material from misguided men out of the Word of Faith fortress in Fort Worth.

I drove off, with both of us in my Maverick, and steered north. I attempted to convince Denny he'd been doing the same thing that our father had, sticking with a woman who could not break free from alcohol. I kept failing. "Denny, you're living your life like Dad and Lou. You're running after an alcoholic, and it will do nothing for you but cause you misery. We can get past this period of your life if you just leave and start over. Listen to me, please."

"No, I don't want to leave. We need to turn back. She's all alone. But you can't stay. You'll have to leave immediately."

"But, Denny, that's how we met Sherelle–at that bar we played on the beach. Neither one of those two women we met had any sort of life. Let her go, please."

Sherelle, and a girlfriend of hers named Carol, had shown up at a corner tavern on Jacksonville Beach one evening while we'd played. The establishment was packed. The proprietor had hired our four-piece country band to play eight consecutive weekend gigs. The women quickly clung to us as they had no place to stay, so I let them spend a couple of days in my rented house on Atlantic Beach, a three-bedroom wood-framed shady place that was the starter home for the owner.

Bruce and I shared his residence for a couple of years before he moved to Douglas, Georgia, to work on a pig farm. I knew Douglas after preaching there once, located a few hours' drive northwest of Jax Beach. The owners were good friends to whom we were introduced after being asked to lead worship one weekend. Bruce took to the farm life well and wanted to return to that rural setting. While absent, he'd let me rent and watch his place.

"Turn this car around right now. I swear I'll hop out at the next stoplight." Denny demanded.

So, I did. I made a U-turn for Austin, dropped Denny off, and drove, instead of north to Chicago, south to Houston, where I knew a couple from one of the church groups I had attended a short time.

Rob and Fran permitted me to stay with them as I sought employment. I held out for a week. Had I known the VA hospital in Houston would have hired me, as I was a Vietnam Era vet with good typing skills, I would have made Houston my home, but instead, I moved on, feeling a better chance existed anywhere but in that steaming hot city.

I called my father and asked for a handout. He was, by then, living in the backwoods of Ohio just across the border from Pennsylvania and married to his third wife. He sent me $100 by telegram, with which I made my way to his 4.5 acres in the tiny country town of Negley.

CHAPTER 29:

At Dad's place

I arrived at Dad's property in Negley, a sparsely populated Ohio village with two lane roads and almost no commercial properties. To the front of Dad's four-and-a-half-acre land he parked an 8 x 12 trailer which he kept for his grandchildren's use. It had a table, a very basic kitchen, a small couch, and a bed and bath. A propane heater kept it warm in the winter, and always, the tank ran out in the early morning hours when the temperature was the coldest. A replacement I had to retrieve thirty yards in front of my small, but very welcome, refuge.

To keep busy during those below freezing December days, I retrieved my typewriter from my Maverick and decided to attempt writing a screenplay. Of all the directions I could have taken, I chose to write an episode for "Little House on the Prairie." It took me about two weeks to complete after which I walked through the snow without boots or winter gear to send my work via the local Mom and Pop store that served as a post office.

A couple of months later, a large manila envelope arrived by mail from NBC in which was a kind letter telling me they appreciated my effort, but at this time, they had plenty of contributors, and besides, Michael Landon did almost all the writing. Still, they were gracious enough to encourage me to get an agent and to continue writing. I was jubilant, thinking, if I did that, I just might land some work for another studio.

While at the store, I got into a conversation with one of the patrons to whom I mentioned my recent graduation from a university with a degree in journalism. She told me of a blind woman living in Youngstown who was writing a book on gardening, of all topics. I adopted that story the moment I noted its potential. I set up a day and time, drove to the woman's house, interviewed her, and wrote the feature.

To the Cleveland Plain Dealer, I sent it. Days later, my father called for me, "David, you're wanted on the phone!"

"Who is it, you know?"

"I didn't ask, but it sounded pretty urgent."

I rushed to pick up the receiver. "This is David."

"We like this feature you wrote about this blind woman and wish to send a photographer to her house to get some shots. Do you have her phone number?"

"Sure, I'll get it right away. It's over in the other trailer. I'll be right back."

I furnished the information and couldn't wait to see my writing in the Dealer. Sure enough, the next Sunday issue, it appeared. With that in hand, as well as the writing I did for the university news, I applied to the Beaver County Times in Beaver, PA, and was hired as one of their correspondents.

For four years, I wrote for the county paper covering the news from local borough city halls, planning commissions, and school board meetings. Also, I submitted features as I came across a subject worthy of note. One such story was of a man who liked to paint Scripture verses on rocks that stuck out of the hillsides in Columbiana County, Ohio. In addition, the paper sent me to cover a church group that was formed by inmates at the county jail. I don't recall if a photographer was assigned to me or not, but I do recall how well the images turned out, as I have all the stories, I wrote for that publication stored in a box in my bedroom.

The big story was when a tornado hit the backside of New Brighton, where three people were killed, houses were destroyed, and a drive-in theater was demolished. The powerful tornado severely damaged or destroyed more than 200 homes and businesses and was the worst natural disaster ever to strike Beaver County. At the north end of the Big Beaver Plaza, an employee and a patron in the state liquor store, who were later identified as Carl Mosketti of Economy, the clerk, and Gladys Brenson of Beaver Falls, became the first fatalities of the still-young twister, crushed by the falling walls of the building. The tornado would continue its destruction for fifty-six miles.

The morning after the touchdown, I was directed to drive to the Beaver County Medical Center to cover the condition of incoming emergency patients. It was both a tragedy as well as an exciting first drama to cover as a newsman. Every one of those articles I wrote for the Times I continue to have in my possession to this day.

CHAPTER 30:

Return to New Brighton

I n between writing jobs, I held positions at other businesses. It began once my father took me along to visit a drinking buddy of his who lived in New Brighton, in southwestern Pennsylvania. He was the same in mill hunky manner as my father, with his strong sarcasm and lack of advanced education showing in the content of his remarks.

His girlfriend, the owner of the two-story home, was attempting to set up a bookstore in the middle of that mill town and as I could see, once I visited her place of business, she struggled to bring in customers. Adding porn, both in magazine and film form, she managed to draw in male patrons, with little attention being given to her meager choice of books.

She soon threw her boyfriend, Rob, out of the house and adopted me as a close friend and eventual lover. After a year, we married, and by that time, I had many shelves built in the store and had gained boxes of books from estate sales which, in a short time, filled the store from one end to the other with a large variety of genres. I encouraged Patti to dispose of the porn, so she called in her supplier, and he retrieved what she had remaining by the cash register. The location had to be there because of the potential for theft. We noticed certain items had gone missing, but no longer in great abundance once the films were set within sight of the checkout counter.

The work at the store, by that time, reached a level to where Patti could keep up with it, but I could tell she was beginning to tire of my always being around once my shift as a pest controller ended at two p.m. She would remind me of tasks needing to be done at the house, none of which were extremely pressing, though worth the effort to get out of the way. One of those jobs included my tearing out the wall in the downstairs bathroom to connect to the adjacent room to create a den.

I learned something of the construction methods in the early 1900s, for rather than sheetrock, the walls were plastered with chicken wire that sunk into the plaster to secure it tightly. Their construction was a much stronger method used in times past, and the outcome left a ton of work for the rebuilder to do once he outlined the size of the hole and drilled through the wall to get through. In no way was it in any way like sheetrock, as the materials were heavier and the walls much thicker, requiring me to cut away the embedded sheets of metal whose plaster broke from the sheets in piles along the bottom of the wall. Once removed, I had to frame the entryway to allow for passage into the room on the other side, which was perfect for our purposes. Inside of that room, I constructed shelving throughout.

The room where all this work took place, the bathroom, also required that every piece of very heavy, dated porcelain be carried outside. The tub alone weighed hundreds of pounds and likely, in the right hands, would have been a true, valuable piece of history. The den I created was used for the store's bookkeeping.

I also completed the construction of shelving in one of the unused bedrooms upstairs. The added shelving helped with the storage of our most treasured books, ones we felt were the most collectible and valuable.

I noticed that any time a certain man from the city came into town to act as if he was searching the shelves for books at the store, Patti came up with a chore for me to do at the house. Not wanting me to be around her intent throughout most of his visits because she liked this man's flirting. I soon discovered he was supplying her with lines of coke that he left on the top of the store's toilet, all lined up and ready for a snort at any time.

I guess Patti decided it was finally time to introduce me to her friend when she permitted him to lead me into the bathroom without telling me what awaited me.

"What's this?" I asked.

He asked me if I ever snorted any coke, to which I replied, "No, although I did a good bit of smoking of hash and opium while I was in the Navy."

"Give it a shot," he said. And so, I did.

My heartbeat jumped to a rate faster than anything I'd ever felt in my whole life. It was experimental to me and scared me at the same time. Everything was moving around me too fast, and I preferred much more mellower sensations than what I experienced.

It was me, this time, who excused myself to go back to the house where I'd be less anxious. I could see now why the fellow's visits were such a treat to Patti. He was an insurance man, if I recall correctly, who had free time during the days when his route took him through New Brighton. He found Patti to be a receptive partier. I never believed she ever got sexually involved with the man, but she later showed me what she was very capable of doing, so now that I look back, I don't doubt anything.

As mentioned, I worked a steady weekday job. It was my most consistent employment and lasted for four years, placing me as the one and only pest management professional for a small Mom and Pop company in the town north of New Brighton–Beaver Falls. It was called Gatto Exterminating, and that connection stabilized me enough to seek sideline work.

The bookstore was doing well, which kept Patti very busy sorting and pricing and motivated me to consider the purchase of a computer. We bought, for an enormous sum of $2,600, one of the first computers, a 386, offered by an elementary-level electronics store in the early 80s.

The store documents could not be composed without using WordPerfect which demanded the use of codes to simply capitalize or cut and paste. A spreadsheet came with a library program we acquired either through the mail or store, as downloading was in its infancy in those days. Despite that, I learned well how to operate the system and showed Patti what I learned, piece by piece. That dinosaur of a computer worked fine for us, and so, as our books gained in number, we added them to or took them from the program, which kept our knowledge of what we had in stock at our fingertips.

As a bassist, I was always playing in one band or another, and after a brief search, I discovered a man who led a wedding band quartet. We often played two weddings per weekend. From most gigs, I earned $60. That rate of pay, sadly, hasn't changed much over the past decades. That was the way with live gigs. There was little space for rising above one's beginnings. These days, gaining a sizable following on YouTube can bring thousands of dollars monthly to a soloist or band.

In addition, as a pest management professional, I sidelined on my own, picking up pest control jobs as a single applicator, and then there was my correspondence gig for the county newspaper on weekday evenings covering various government meetings for five boroughs out of the 52 boroughs and townships.

The economy showed signs of slowing to a near halt, so, in response, Patti insisted we sell everything and relocate to Florida, to St. Petersburg, where her newly married girlfriend resided. We made the move after an enormous amount of preparation, but by then, our marriage began to suffer because of Patti's continual lies and hiding of facts.

My writing for local daily and weekly publications in Pennsylvania didn't want to manifest in Florida no matter how hard I tried. The St. Petersburg Times evening edition, called The Evening Independent, hired me to cover one city hall meeting, then let me go after a few days because the company chose to drop the evening paper entirely. They too, were beginning to see the writing on the wall when it came to journalism careers. The industry was headed for computer broadcasts and websites. Soon, no one would get news-papers thrown on their lawns in the morning. That ritual soon bit the dust.

I went from holding down four jobs in Pennsylvania to struggling to find one in Florida. The decline of the newspaper industry was upon us. Oh, I did find work covering all the stories contained in a weekly free paper in Madeira Beach, but even that paper closed shop due to its compulsive drunken publisher. So, I searched for whatever I could to help pay the bills and landed on three months of steady weekly music work playing with an Elvis impersonator until, as bands always do, it folded. The head of the band refused to pay me for two straight weeks of gigs at which time I drove to his house with a baseball bat in my hand insisting he hand me my money. I was paid then and there and was fired while setting up my equipment at our next Steak 'n Ale gig.

CHAPTER 31:

New Start in Tampa

P atti and I divorced in 1988. It hurt me and caused me emotional problems for many years. Still, I kept praying and hoping for a turnaround in my life, a revival. It was a terrible, lengthy period of heartache and pain, even while I was experiencing the most difficult time finding gainful employment in St. Petersburg. Where I was located wasn't working for me. I moved to Tampa where my brother put me up for a few months. Soon afterward, I moved into a house with an old man in his three-bedroom home in Temple Terrace. His compulsive whistling drove me out of my mind.

Near to this man's house was the VA hospital, where, one day, I walked into the personnel office, told them I was a Vietnam Era vet, and that I could type. In those days, 45 WPM was a sought-after achievement, so personnel hired me to type forms for their prosthetic service on the ground floor. Over a year later, the Nursing Service heard about me from one of the women in the office and asked if I'd join their team. I did. Keeping my eyes on the medical center's job openings, I noticed two years later that the hospital sought a replacement for their pest controller, as they called him. I applied, was hired, and remained in that position for thirty years, even as it grew in wages and responsibilities. It became my ticket to the ownership of a house, a car, and a retirement savings plan called TSP.

CHAPTER 32:

Moving On

A round the mid-80s, while in family dysfunction therapy, I began to step away and gain some distance, which helped me to understand the influences that surrounded men out of the 50s-80s union culture. Perhaps from their hard work, heat, and limited education, these men adopted strong vulgarity, racism, brutality, alcoholism, and distorted, one-sided views. The talks in the mills were filled with black humor and mean-spirited wit, and fathers took this same culture home with them, transforming themselves into being selfish, unaffectionate, emotionally blocked, and despisers of academics.

It is my desire to see a great change transpire within groups of men who associate so intensely with one another, such as members within labor unions. There is indeed a culture that arises out of those groups that is not often for the betterment of the workplace or the family. For change to take place, members must choose to be aware of their contributions to their brand of bigotry and a jolly vulgarity that does little to aid family relations. It is not corny to think love, joy, peace, longsuffering, gentleness, meekness, temperance, and goodness should take the lead in attitudes and conversations, even in the most strength-challenging toil. It is mature to desire change. Bearing good fruits strengthens, not weakens, the hearts and minds of individuals. It comes time to lay aside the former and follow kindness.

"Yet man is born into trouble as the sparks fly upward," we are reminded in Job 5:7. There is no escaping the hard times. Maybe my life has more seasons to move in and out of, for, as we have all heard many times before, the only certainty in life is change. It can contain good seasons and bad seasons. For me, it was from one location to another, each with its own set of challenges. Sure, there were good times, and there were hard times, even a horrific event. And yet, I had to move on, putting one foot in front of the other as I learned to put my trust in God, to "look for a city which has foundations, whose builder and maker is God." (Hebrews 11:10)

The kind of family dysfunction that is born out of sarcastic, alcoholic and bigoted millwork saturated communities is one of the toughest mental cages to break free of. Relations at home become sheer madness, I learned early. Sadly, the only true rescue for many suffering the lifestyle is the total abandonment of one's family of origin. That is not the best answer. Still, it remains a choice. My solution is for families to adopt listening skills, learn to forgive and forget, and realize, though madness exists, one must press on to wholeness by God's grace.

WORKS CITED

Charismatic Abuses? Doctrinal and Emotional by John Piper found at
youtube.com/results?search_query=john+piper+on+doctrinal+abuses+in+the+Charismatic+Church

The Worst Military Experience//BOOT CAMP STORIES by Austen
Alexander at https://www.facebook.com/austenalexanderpublic